St Andrews

The Old Course & Open Champions

DAVID JOY *Historian / Illustrator*

IAIN MACFARLANE LOWE *Photographer*

KYLE PHILLIPS *Golf Course Architect*

Published in 2006 by
Iain Lowe Photography Ltd
10 Fergusson Place
St Andrews
Fife KY16 9NF

ISBN   0-9552393-0-3

                    978-0-9552393-0-4

Bobby Locke:
Open Champion at St Andrews 1957

Seve Ballesteros:
Open Champion at St Andrews 1984

St Andrews by the Northern Sea,
A haunted town it is to me!
A little city, worn and grey,
The grey North Ocean girds it
round,
And o'er the rocks and up the bay,
The long sea-rollers surge and
sound.
And still the thin and biting spray
Drives down the melancholy street,
And still endure, and still decay,
Towers that the salt winds vainly
beat.
Ghost-like and shadowy they stand
Dim mirrored in the wet sea sand.

Andrew Laing (1814-1912)

Aerial view from St Andrews Bay of the town and its linksland.

After the successful formatting of "Scottish Golf Links – a Photographer's Journey" – Iain Macfarlane Lowe has teamed up again with David Joy for his historical commentary and Kyle Philips for architectural observations in this strikingly–illustrated new book on St Andrews - The Old Course and its Champions.

David Joy is a born and bred St Andrean whose great–grandfather was one of Tom Morris's registered caddies in the 1890s. Joy is best known internationally for his portrayal of Tom Morris "The Grand Old Man of Golf" both on stage and screen. As a highly-respected golf historian his comments bring to life the unique history of the game in St Andrews. Also an artist, all the line drawings in this book are from his own hand and add an extra dimension to this look at St Andrews and its champions.

Iain Macfarlane Lowe is an internationally recognised golf course photographer. In conjunction with David Joy in "St Andrews and the Open Championship – the Official History", his photographs featured strongly in showing the Old Course in all its moods. In this book he has taken his task even further and captured the whole essence of the course and the antiquity of "The Old Grey City of St Andrews".

Kyle Philips is a world-renowned golf course architect whose sketches and comments on each hole on the Old Course give reason to why it is held in such high esteem. Based in Granite Bay, California, he has over 25 years of experience in top-class course design behind him. With a portfolio stretching across five continents his international reputation has grown from successes in America, Holland, Italy, Austria and South Africa. In the United Kingdom, Kingsbarns Golf Links near St Andrews was one of Kyle's designs which was much acclaimed and immediately ranked among the top 50 courses in the world in 2001. More recently his successes at The Grove, near London, and Dundonald near Glasgow have continued to prove his unique talent.

CONTENTS

St Andrews

The Old Course & Open Champions

THE ORIGINAL BIG THREE

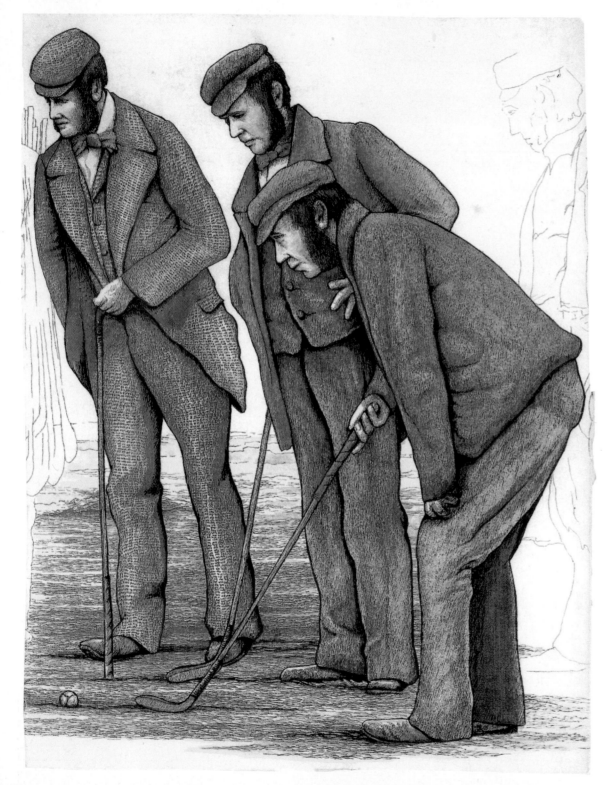

St Andrews 1857

Left to right:

WILLIE PARK

The first Open Champion, who won four times in 1860, '63, '66 and '75.

TOM MORRIS

Keeper of the Green at Prestwick 1851 –'64. Open Champion 1861, '62, '64 and '67 and Custodian of the Links of St Andrews 1864 to 1902.

ALLAN ROBERTSON

Known as "The world's first golf professional" was reputed to have never been beaten. Died in 1859, one year before the Open Championship started.

ST ANDREWS
A Royal and Ancient City

When the old grey town is shrouded in mist, with its ancient spires and towers breaking the horizon, images and echoes of its long and volatile past are conjured up. Kings and cardinals, martyrs and reformers, merchants, provosts, pilgrims and scholars have all left their mark and helped to shape its unique history over the past nine hundred years.

Six centuries ago, that famous strip of linksland where the Old Course now lies, was known as "Muckross", a Pictish name meaning "headland of swine". King David I gifted the land to the people of St Andrews in the year the foundation stone was laid for the cathedral (1120). It was a way of compensating the locals for the disruption the construction of this huge building would cause in the heart of their town and twenty years later the King also declared it a Royal Burgh. St Andrews, having changed from its old name of "Kilrymont", prospered with its status as the ecclesiastical capital and first seat of learning in Scotland. With the magnificent cathedral (consecrated by Robert the Bruce in 1318), and university (founded in 1410), pilgrims flocked to St Andrews to see relics of the saint it was named after. It became a walled city, where a pass was needed to enter. Even the young kings James II and III were schooled in the castle, perched over the North Sea in the shadow of the square tower.

The Reformation was a stormy and dramatic affair which culminated in the ransacking and torching of the cathedral in 1559; this not only tore the heart out of the city, but instantly bankrupted it. For nearly three centuries it was to lie doleful and idle.

The Victorian era and the fast-growing interest in playing golf were to see the city raise its profile once again. 1850 was the turning point, when a railway line linked the town to points north, south and west, making the course accessible to all. The final incentive to golf at St Andrews was that the hand-stitched feather ball was replaced by the cheaper solid gutta. Suddenly the course was accessible and the ball affordable. Visitors increased each year but were never charged for a round of golf in St Andrews until the late 1920s. The town council were just content to attract holiday makers and increase the town's economy, which it has done in no uncertain terms ever since!

The ruins of St Andrews Cathedral – once the ecclesiastical capital of Scotland, founded in 1120, consecrated by Robert The Bruce in 1318, plundered and destroyed during the Reformation in 1559.

The original parchment granting Archbishop Hamilton permission to breed cuniggus (rabbits) on the links as long as he did not interfere with the locals rights to play foote-ball and gowf: issued by the council of the City of St Andrews and dated 15th January 1552. (Shown left)

A map of the town dated 1580. Its three main streets (North St, Market St and South St), constructed in the twelfth century, run parallel to each other and lead towards the Cathedral entrance.

The ruins of St Andrews Castle which housed and schooled the young kings of Scotland in the 15th century. During the reigns of James 11, 111 and IV, Acts of Parliament were posted banning "foote-ball and gowf" being played on the Sabbath (Sunday) as it interfered with their archery practise – which was crucial to the Defence of the Realm!

Sir Hugh Lyon Playfair played a huge part in the resurrection of the old grey town, which lay dormant and decaying in the first part of the nineteenth century. As Chief Magistrate and Provost in 1843 he literally took the town and its inhabitants by the scruff of the neck and knocked them back into shape! An ex-Lieutenant Colonel of the Bombay Lancers with inherent wealth, he started his campaign to clean up the town in 1843 with "forty rules and regulations that must be obeyed" - eg: "You will not be allowed to accumulate more than one ton of manure on your premises between the months of May to September inclusive". Sir Hugh was formidable and worked tirelessly to improve and promote the image of St Andrews. He supervised the construction of three streets, creating an ambience similar to opulent Georgian Edinburgh, to attract people of wealth and status to the town. He was instrumental in building the R & A Clubhouse (1854) and the Town Hall. Sir Hugh organised the construction of a railway to join up with the main line three miles from the town – he even bought the train to go with it!

Sir Hugh Lyon Playfair

"THE KING OF CLUBS" 1815 to 1859

In the cathedral grounds, on one side of Allan Robertson's grave is carved out two crossed clubs and balls, and a ribbon with the inscription "Far And Sure". When he died in 1859 he was described as "the greatest golf – player that ever lived, of whom alone in the annals of the past-time it can be said that he was never beaten". He had been a feather ball maker, as were his father and grandfather before him, all exceptional golfers and unofficial unpaid professionals to the Royal and Ancient Golf Club, although Allan was said to be the best of them.

In September, 1858 Allan Robertson was the first to break 80 on The Old Course. It was considered near miraculous at the time, considering the clubs used to swipe hand hammered "gutta" balls on a course that was unforgiving – mainly due to the lack of maintenance on it. The fairways were narrow, the gorse was thick and the rough – rough! His best eclectic score in such conditions for the Old Course was 56, 27 out (helped by a hole in one at the 8th) and 29 back. He was slight in build, and only 5ft 4ins tall, but was never seen to force a shot – letting the whip of the shaft on those old heavy faced goose-necks do the work for him. When Allan Robertson died, Prestwick decided to instigate a competition to see who would take over his mantle as the undisputed "Champion Golfer" – which was to be the first Open, played in 1860.

This monument erected as a memorial after the sad demise of Young Tom Morris in 1875, was paid for by subscription from all of the sixty clubs in existence at that time. Thirty-three years later "Old Tom" was laid to rest beside his family, having survived them all – his wife, three sons and daughter – and just 30 yards from his old playing partner Allan Robertson. Between them lies Willie Auchterlonie and his son Laurie – both Honorary Professionals to the R & A. Within the cathedral grounds six past Open Champions are laid to rest.

The cathedral end of North Street with its fishermen's quarters, photographed from St Salvators steeple in 1848.

An aerial view showing that all roads lead to or from the Cathedral Ruins! On the coastline, to the right, can be seen the Castle ruins with the R & A and Old Course beyond.

This aerial view shows the charm and character of the buildings and town houses in the heart of the city. To the extreme left is the main university library - a building which, from the air, looks out of context compared to its surroundings. Thankfully this large facility is hidden away at street level and does not spoil the ambience of St Salvator's steeple and its quadrangle. To the right, behind Younger Hall, are housed many of the university's older faculties and residencies.

S t Andrews "Ancient and Modern". University science buildings and student residences flank the right-hand side of the approach to The Old Course and the main entrance to the town.

This heraldic crest featuring St Andrew is part of an impressive entrance to Lower College Hall in the quadrangle of St Salvator's – one of the oldest parts of the University in North Street.

THE YOUNGER HALL

The Younger Hall was built, for St Andrews University, through the generosity of the Younger family (brewers) in 1920. Above the main entrance are carved the names of the University Rector at that time – Nansen, the explorer, and its Chancellor, Earl Haig. Another great benefactor of the University was Andrew Carnegie (Rector 1901-1907) who, from Fife, had gone over to America and made his fortune in the steel industry. His donations provided a library, scholarships and playing fields.

The Younger Hall, next door to College Gate and St Salvator's in North Street, has hosted some grand affairs. It is used for graduation ceremonies, balls, exams and concerts. Bobby Jones received the Freedom of the City in 1958 and in recent times past Champions Jack Nicklaus, Gary Player, Peter Thomson, Seve Ballesteros and Nick Faldo were all awarded honorary degrees on its stage.

In the shadow of its steeple, students congregate in the quadrangle of St Salvators College. Founded by Bishop Kennedy in 1450, it was intended for "the teaching of theology and arts, for divine worship and scholastic exercise, and for the strengthening of the orthodox heretics".

On the cobbles at the entrance through the steeple to the quadrangle are the initials PH. Patrick Hamilton had come to St Andrews to compose music in the cathedral and study theology. As an outspoken Lutheran he was soon in trouble and ended his short life burnt at the stake for heresy on this very spot. Above, on the steeple wall, it is said that his head mysteriously appeared carved in stone after he was torched, thus enhancing his martyrdom! It is considered unlucky for students to walk over the initials during exam times.

St Salvator's steeple – a familiar landmark on the home holes of the Old Course. When in doubt a caddie would point to the skyline and say to his man, "Just aim on the steeple Sir!" Its original name in Old Scots was "Sanct Salvatour" meaning "dedicated to the Holy Saviour".

Gargoyles and heraldic crests loom large and imposing throughout the older parts of the University and the town.

ST LEONARD'S CHAPEL

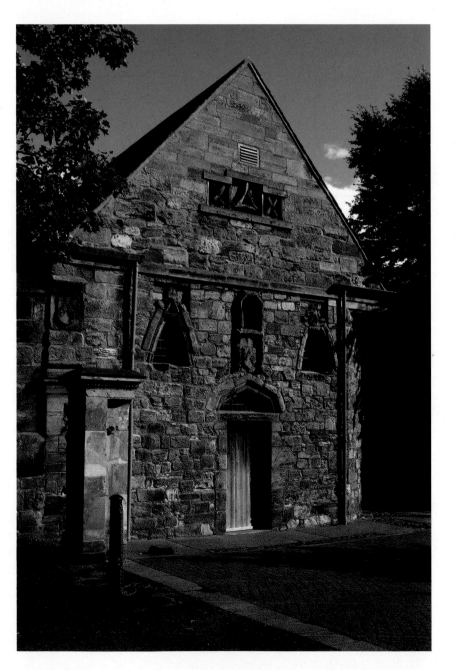

The grounds of St Leonard's are even bigger than the Cathedral's next door. It housed some grand buildings both private and public. St Leonard's College was founded within its grounds in 1512. Mary Queen of Scots stayed in what is now part of St Leonard's School library. Her brother had a house there and she was delighted to be "a bourgeoisie" as often as she could in St Andrews in the 1560s. Mary is probably the first woman to play golf on the St Andrews Links. She was spotted, just one week after the mysterious murder of her husband Lord Darnley, "gowfing" on the links of Seton near Edinburgh, which aroused suspicions! The Chapel, re-roofed and refurbished in recent years, now belongs to the University. At one time it was a "Hospitium" or almshouse for "women of little fruit, either of devoutness or virtue".

This oil of "Gentlemen at Play" dated 1740, painted just fourteen years before the R & A was founded, now hangs in the reading room of the club. Although St Andrews was known as "the Metropolis of Golf" during the seventeenth and eighteenth centuries, there were surprisingly few people playing. Those who were profiled were men of property or inherent wealth Gentlemen who had the leisure time to partake in recreation on the links!

In this painting, the action looks as if it's well out on the course, but it is in fact not far up what is now the 2nd fairway. The Swilken Bridge is to the right with Methven's Tower on the hill behind – now by the site of Martyrs' Monument which stands directly behind the Royal & Ancient Clubhouse (built in 1854).

When the R & A held its first meeting they congregated outside the Tollbooth by Stewart's Hotel (now The Cross Keys), on the cobbled end of Market Street, to be piped down to the course for the start of play at 10 am. This tradition was maintained during their annual Spring and Autumn meetings for over seventy years, until the construction of Golf Place. A clubhouse was then acquired – "The Old Union Parlour", situated behind the 18th green: as seen on the next page.

(Oil Painting 1740)

Above: The first photograph of the Old Course, 1849

1. The Old Union Parlour.

2 .Allan Robertson's cottage where feather balls were made.

3. Hugh Philip's (club maker) workshop.

4. Communal drying green.

5 .Lifeboat Shed – the road across the 1st and 18th fairway was created by

pulling the lifeboat across the course.

The Old Union Parlour, 1850

Comparing the first photograph of "The Home Hole" to a recent one, Hamilton Hall (originally The Grand Hotel) built in 1896 now stands on the site of the two cottages to the left of the Old Union Parlour. The Parlour's frontage still looks the same and is now used for the R & A's Open Championship offices. Hugh Philp's workshop is now the Tom Morris Golf Shop, and the communal drying green and lifeboat shed is Rusacks Hotel built in 1891. The R & A Clubhouse was constructed and in use five years after this old photograph was taken in 1849.

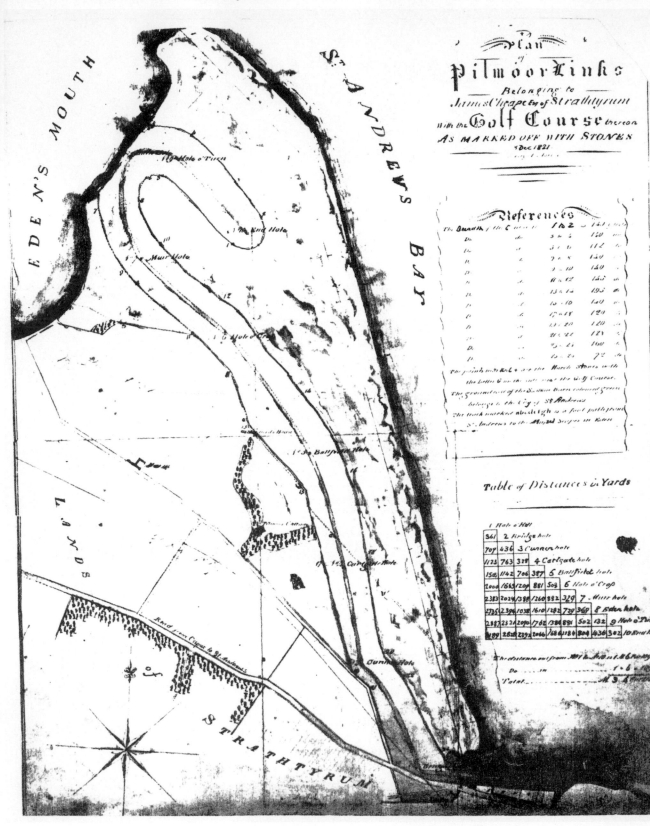

This map, charted in 1821, shows the original nine holes of the Old Course, known at that time as the Pilmoor Links. When the St Andrews Society of Golfers (later to be known as The Royal and Ancient Golf Club) were formed in 1754, they played a Spring and Autumn meeting around an eleven hole course. After ten years it was decided at a club meeting that the first four holes were too short and should be merged into two, thus the established nine hole course was formed, playing out to the estuary and playing the same holes back to the town, inward players having the right of way.

The course evolved, rather than was constructed, and after centuries of use in "taking recreation", breeding rabbits, tending sheep and cattle, the course emerged through well trodden pathways and hazards created by sheltering animals avoiding hostile winter winds and rain.

Spectators around the last green in "The Grand Tournament" of 1857

A grandstand view of the 18th tee during the Millennium Open

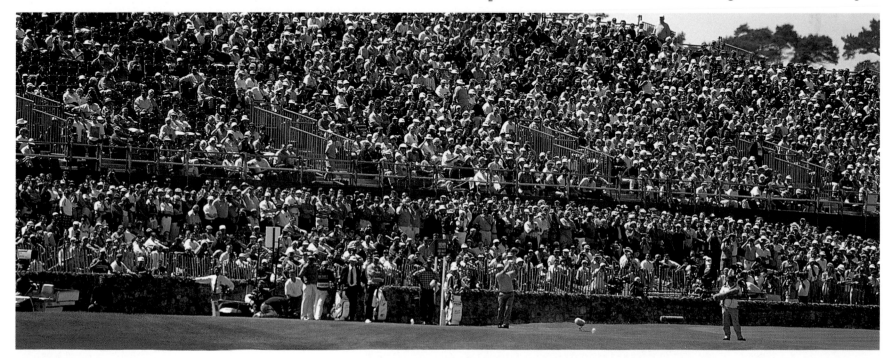

THE CHAMPIONSHIP "Big Three" Of The 1850s and 1860s

Left to right: Willie Park, the first winner of The Open in 1860 representing Musselburgh, won again in 1863, '66 and '75. Tom Morris Senior, runner-up in the first Open and winner in 1861, '62 and '64 is still recognised as the oldest winner at the age of forty-six in 1867. His son, "Young Tom", won his first of four Opens aged seventeen in 1868, and again in 1869, '70 and '72. All of their wins were at Prestwick.

TOM MORRIS

Morris Snr 1861

Tom Morris, having spent thirteen years at Prestwick, was invited back to the home of his birth to be custodian of the Links of St Andrews, or "Keeper of the Green" in 1864. Having been presented with his emblems of office, a bucket, barrow and a spade, he became responsible for all the major changes on the Old Course over a period of forty years.

Born in 1821, he started his career as a feather ball maker with Allan Robertson, making two a day from a cottage by the 18th green. In a good year in the 1840s, two thousand balls would be stitched up. Morris, partnering Robertson, was never beaten in two ball foursomes (which was the main game of that time) from 1842 until Allan's untimely death in 1859.

Tom Morris played in thirty-six consecutive Opens and had mammoth battles against Willie Park in the 1850s – challenges, not over thirty-six holes, but thirty-six rounds! – twelve at North Berwick – twelve at Musselburgh and twelve at St Andrews, over three weeks, with the two Sundays used as travel time between venues!! A normal challenge match at that time was twelve rounds in six days' play. Morris had a swim every day of his working life wherever he could find a bit of water – three strokes out and four strokes back!

Tom Morris in his 80th year

By the time Tom Morris retired in 1902 he was known nationally as "The Grand Old Man of Golf". He had lived through the major changes in the evolution of the game: from trains linking up the linksland in the 1840s and the feather ball being replaced by the more affordable "gutta" - to the first Opens in the 1860s - to courses and clubs being established throughout the country in the 1870s and '80s - to the1890s, when he laid out greens from the Northern Isles of Scotland to the southern coast of England and over the sea to the linksland of Ireland.

In his twilight years, he was reassured as to how established and popular the game had become. Old Tom died just three weeks short of his eighty-seventh birthday in 1908.

ST ANDREWS GOLFING LINKS

New course
3rd Fairway

16th Fairway & Green

17th
Jubilee Course
2nd

"Seven Sisters" Bunkers   5th Fairway   "Hell" Bunker and 14th & 4th Double Green
The Old Course

The Old Course
16th Green

2nd tee & 1st Green
Eden Course

THE ST ANDREWS OPEN CHAMPIONS
Comments by David Joy

After the first twelve years of The Open being played at Prestwick, Tom Kidd, a local man and part-time caddie, won on his home patch, the Old Course, in 1873. Another St Andrean, Bob Martin, also a caddie and clubmaker with Tom Morris, followed in his footsteps by winning in 1876 and bettered Kidd by lifting the trophy again in 1885. Between these two wins came Jamie Anderson, a local clubmaker, and Bob Ferguson from Musselburgh. Having left the town to become a professional in England, Jack Burns returned to claim the Claret Jug in 1888. After yet another St Andrews man, Hugh Kirkaldy, beat his brother by two shots in 1891, the championship expanded. To keep up with the growing interest nationally, two courses in England were added to the circuit and "The Triumvirate" of Vardon, Taylor and Braid emerged to dominate proceedings until the outbreak of the First World War. Although Harry Vardon (still the six times record holder of The Open), didn't win on the Old Course, his colleagues did. Englishman J. H. Taylor won back to back in 1895 and 1900, as did Scotsman James Braid in 1905 and 1910.

From the 1920s the Americans sailed over "the pond" and back again with the trophy on twelve out of thirteen occasions. The first of these was Jock Hutchison in 1921, who was in fact a St Andrean who had emigrated to the USA six years before and taken American citizenship. Probably the most popular winner at St Andrews was Bobby Jones in 1927, followed by fellow countryman Densmore Shute in 1933. Englishman Dick Burton stopped the American dominance in 1939 but, after the disruption of the Second World War, Sam Snead came over in 1946 and won comfortably.

As a born and bred St Andrean (fourth generation) I have been fortunate to have witnessed the last eleven Opens played here:- from vague memories of crowds in 1955 as a six-year-old boy, to the excitement of a flash flood disrupting play in the Centenary Open - to recent times and watching the emotional parade of past champions playing the first and last two holes of the course prior to the Millennium Championship.

The 1950s saw Australian Peter Thomson and South African Bobby Locke claim the title in "The Home of Golf". The Centenary Open, in 1960, marked the development of an international interest in the

Jock Jutchison 1921

championship, assisted by television and Arnold Palmer!! The charismatic Palmer was runner-up to Australian Kel Nagle. "Champagne" Tony Lema waltzed away with the 1964 Open, beating fellow countryman Jack Nicklaus into second place by five shots. Nicklaus became one of only four double winners with a play off win against Doug Sanders in 1970 and a successful defence of his title at St Andrews when it returned in 1978.

Has there ever been a win with more sense of theatre about it than Ballesteros and his "ole'" gesture in 1984? His birdie putt dropped on the last green to deny Tom Watson of his chance to equal Vardon's long-held record of six wins. In 1990 Nick Faldo gave Britain only its second win at St Andrews since 1910 when he ground out an emphatic win! John Daly, after the first four-hole play off on the Old Course, coped with the blustery conditions to emerge victorious in 1995. Finally, Tiger Woods mastered the course in the Millennium Open, and again when it returned in 2005, with a display of control and skill worthy of joining that elite band of double winners on the Old Course.

Above: Jock Hutchison, the 1921 winner, was the first American to win at St Andrews but a born–and–bred St Andrean!

THE OLD COURSE
Architectural comments by
Kyle Phillips

Never has a course been more beautifully woven together into a single golfing canvas than the Old Course of St Andrews. Even the man-made elements and activities of the town, shops and a public road known as Granny Clark's Wynd, interacting with the opening and finishing holes create an ambience that is not to be found anywhere else in golf.

The strategic intertwining of the fairways is unsurpassed. The scale and majesty of its greens cannot be matched. So sophisticated is the design, it is completely understandable how its brilliance can be misunderstood in a single round. But, as with all great works of art, its complexities are only to be revealed and fully appreciated by those connoisseurs of architecture who take the time to study it carefully. It is, quite simply, the oldest existing example of a golf course laid out on naturally-formed links terrain, which still provides challenge and excitement for all levels of golfers.

The most important design rule to keep in mind as one plays the Old Course is there are no rules. The Old Course is a continuous loop of holes that in years past alternated direction of play regularly. Today the holes are played in a counter-clockwise sequence. However, during the first few days in April each year, the course can played in a clockwise direction.

I find most people who have played the Old Course only once or twice, have difficulty remembering holes 2 through 6 and 13 through 16. This is partially because the course has only one par 5 and one par 3 on each nine and partially because both of these stretches of holes all play continuously in the same direction over similar terrain.

As is borne out in the way the design of the course has evolved, this is really a one-way course with two-way traffic. Keeping this fact in mind will help one to remember that every par 4 plays parallel to another par 4, as do the two par 5's and two par 3's. The total number of these parallel holes will always total 19 (i.e., hole 5 plays parallel to hole 14). In addition, every double green will always equal 18 (i.e., green 6 is shared with green 12). The geometry of the course is fascinating. My first experience with the Old Course came from the commanding viewpoint of the upper level office of the then Royal & Ancient Secretary, Sir Michael Bonallack. Stationed at his periscope, he told me that the widest point on the course was not more than 450 feet.

Occupying a thrifty 96 acres, the majority of the double fairway course is played through a corridor that is less than 400 feet wide, with the narrowest point a scant 240 feet wide. When one compares this to other championship courses of 150-180 acres, one starts to imagine the close proximity of the tees and greens as well as the tightness of the out-of-bounds. Ironically, the greens are the largest in the game of golf. The double greens average over 40,000 square feet in size. Even when the total area of the greens is divided by 18, they still average over 20,000 square feet, which is over three times the size of typical greens designed today. The scale of these massive greens allow for an abundance of pin positions, separated by natural flowing humps and hollows.

The Old Course is influenced by generations of golfing history. For example, in the original rules of golf, the teeing ground was within one club length from the previous hole. In many instances the Old Course teeing grounds are simply an extension of the greens. In order to preserve the challenge of original landing areas, new Championship tees have been added further back and away from the previous green, but for mere mortals these adjacent teeing grounds are still in use today.   While the recent history of the Old Course has been to defend against technology primarily by adding length to the course, there is no more room. In fact, the 2005 Open Championship Course was actually played not only on the Old Course, but on parts of two adjacent courses, as well as the Himalayas (Ladies) Putting Green. Unless a lid is placed on technology, future defences will require rethinking additional aspects of the course and would certainly include significant and certainly controversial changes to bunker and green designs.

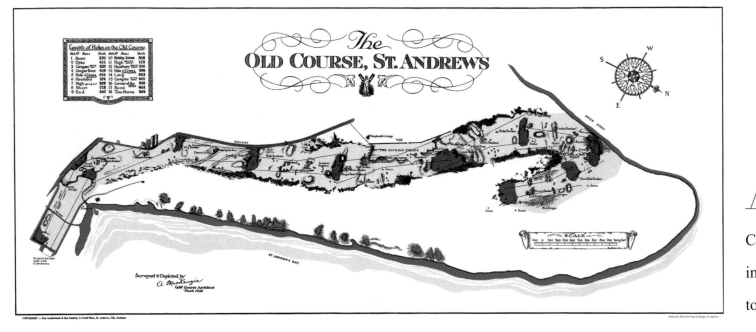

Alistair Mackenzie's map of the Old Course (March 1924) hang in the office of the Secreta to the R & A.

1st

"Burn"

376 yard par 4

1873 - The Old Course plays host to the
first Open Championship in St Andrews.

Hole #1 - "Burn"

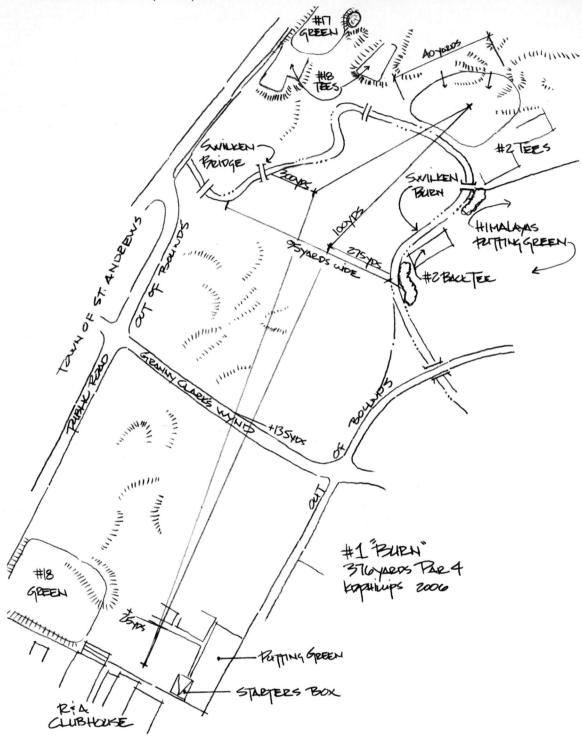

Starting from the shadows of the Royal & Ancient Golf Club and the town of St. Andrews, this opening hole gives a false sense of security. Even though over 120 yards of expansive fairway awaits, the lack of rough and the tightly mown, firm, fast surface of the links brings a tee shot leaked to the right quickly out of bounds or into the Swilken Burn.

As this designer knows all too well, over-compensation for the hazards on the right, can result in finding the out-of-bounds or Swilken Burn down the left. A good strategy is to play over Granny Clark's Wynd to the 100-yard area just near the entry of the Swilken horseshoe. The Swilken Burn guards the front of this large 40 yard deep green, and immediately right of the adjacent 2nd tee is the out-of-bound Himalayas Putting Green.

Architectural Sketch & Comments by Kyle Phillips

The Old Course 1st and 18th fairway which, flanked by out-of-bounds, has no bunkers.

TOM KIDD
1st Winner

An aerial view of the 1st green protected, to the front, by the Swilken Burn.

On the 4th October 1873, The Open was played on the Old Course for the first time. Having acquired more ground in 1870, the course had been altered to accommodate eighteen holes and played "the modern way" – anti-clockwise, rather than on the traditional clockwise circuit of the original nine holes.

At ten o'clock, on that Saturday morning, Mr D. McWhannel and Mr Henry Lamb had the honour of teeing off first, followed by defending champion, Young Tom Morris. A large crowd gathered in anticipation of a record fifth win in a row over the two eighteen hole rounds of the day. Old Tom, still in contention although in his fifty-third year, was one of the twenty-six competitors in the field. It was disappointing that the Park brothers and a few other notable professionals had not made the journey over.

Some of the crack amateur players, having just competed in the R & A Autumn meeting, made up the numbers.

It was unexpected when Tom Kidd, a local caddie, emerged as the winner with rounds of 91 and 88. It was to be the highest aggregate until four rounds were introduced at Muirfield in 1892. It was deflating for Kidd to read in the press that – quote – "It was scarcely anticipated that he would carry off the palm. As a player he is likely to improve." To be fair, he was popular amongst his fellow competitors and was not exactly a two round wonder! Kidd was a lively twenty-four-year old, who gave the ball a good "swipe". He had won high-profile challenge matches that year partnering David Strath against the Morris's and the Park brothers.

Tom Kidd

Conditions in that first St Andrews Open were favourable, but there were puddles, large and small, throughout the fairways after four days of constant rain. With no preferred lies being one of the basic thirteen rules being adhered to, it must be presumed that the odds-on favourite, Tom Morris, had wet feet and a heavy heart by the end of the day's play!

Tom Morris Jnr with the Challenge belt, which he kept after three consecutive wins while still a teenager in 1870: five years later he was dead! On Christmas day, aged twenty-four, his sad demise had followed the equally tragic death of both his wife and first-born in childbirth just three months before.

Young Tom's grief was insurmountable and it was commonly thought that he died of a broken heart. Old Tom was heard to say plaintively later in life, that if that had been true, then he wouldn't be around either.

2nd

"Dyke"

453 yard par 4

In between Bob Martin's double win at
St Andrews in 1876 and '85, Jamie Anderson and
Bob Ferguson added their names to the Claret Jug.

Hole #2 – "Dyke"

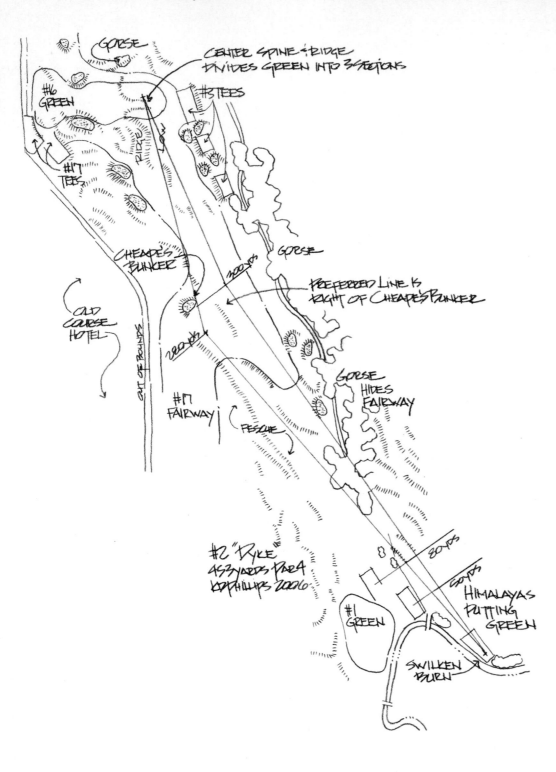

GORSE

CENTER SPINE & RIDGE
DIVIDES GREEN INTO 3 SECTIONS

#6
GREEN

#3 TEES

RIDGE

LOW

#7
TEES

CHEAPE'S
BUNKER

200 YDS

GORSE

OLD
COURSE
HOTEL

OUT OF BOUNDS

PREFERRED LINE IS
RIGHT OF CHEAPE'S BUNKER

220 YDS

#17
FAIRWAY

FESCUE

GORSE
HIDES
FAIRWAY

#2 "DYKE"
453 YARDS PAR 4
KYLE PHILLIPS 2006

#1
GREEN

80 YDS

SWILKEN
BURN

60 YDS

HIMALAYAS
PUTTING
GREEN

I n stark contrast to the opening hole, the drive on the 2nd plays blind, obscured by gorse bushes. This, like many of the drives at the Old Course, favours a drive left off the tee to avoid the gorse down the right. Beware of "Cheape's" bunker on the left awaiting drives that attempt to get within 150 yards of the green. The further left off the tee the more difficult the contours leading into the green make the approach. Magnificent humps and rolls extend into the green to turn and deflect running approaches, as well as creating mind-boggling chip shots from near the green.

Architectural Sketch & Comments by Kyle Phillips

This obscured view of the fairway from the second tee is typical of all tees on the way out, until the 8th. When playing the Old Course for the first time, a caddie is a great asset in advising on what line to take on most of its holes.

Gorse, rough ground and bunkers discourage a drive down the right side of the 2nd. Cheapes Bunker (pictured), to the left of the fairway; is a hazard that gathers many long drives. Playing out of this bunker can be most uncomfortable at times, as shown by the golfer with his right foot in it and sitting on his left foot outside the bunker.

Bob Martin was a registered caddie and club-maker with Tom Morris. He had been runner-up to Willie Park at Prestwick in 1875, but went one better on his home patch the following year. He became the first of five double winners of The Open on the Old Course, having won again in 1885.

Through its long and dramatic history, 1876 was the most controversial of any Open played. It got off to a bad start when, because of the excitement or disruption of Prince Leopold's visit that week as the Captain of the Royal and Ancient, the secretary of the club had forgotten to book tee times for The Open Championship and the competitors had to play off between members playing their Autumn meeting! The outcome was even more unsatisfactory when David Strath, who thought he had won, was penalised for an infringement on the 17th, and told that he would have to play Martin over eighteen holes to decide the outcome. He refused and Bob Martin walked the course the following Monday to be declared the winner!! It was less traumatic in 1885, when Martin was loudly applauded coming down the last hole into a stiff breeze, five shots better than he had been on his previous win against the ill-fated David Strath. In 1879 Strath died of consumption, as had his brother, who had won the Championship in 1865.

Bob Martin, the first double winner of The Open at St Andrews

The Andersons were a well-known St Andrews golfing family and none more so than Jamie Anderson, who was the first to win three consecutive Opens on the three course circuit: Musselburgh in 1877, Prestwick in 1878 and St Andrews in 1879. He did not defend the championship at Musselburgh the following year, as he said he was not notified in time!

Anderson had played in The Opens at Prestwick from 1866 – '70 and was just beaten by one shot in the first championship at St Andrews. He was admired for his skill in the use of the "approaching iron", (a links-type bump and run). He had started his career, like many others, as an apprentice club maker with Forgans. This factory was to become the largest manufacturer of hickory clubs in the world, up until the transition to steel shafts in 1928.

His father "Daw" Anderson, had been "keeper of the green" on the Old Course for a short time until Tom Morris took over in 1864. "Daw" then caddied for Morris for nearly forty years. During this time he ran the ginger beer stand situated on the 4th tee and served refreshments to whoever passed him by. (see illustration on page 73).

When Anderson won at St Andrews on Saturday, 4 October 1879, twenty-three couples teed off. Thirty-six professionals and ten amateurs played for a purse of £55.00. Ten pounds was awarded to the winner, and a medal, which he would have to pay himself to have engraved.

Jamie Anderson – triple winner

ob Ferguson, representing Musselburgh, followed Anderson's feat of winning three in a row in 1880, '81 and '82 at Musselburgh, Prestwick and St Andrews. If Willie had not holed "a tram liner" on the last green in an eighteen hole play-off the following year back at Musselburgh, he would have won four!

His win on the Old Course started with a round of 83, four shots clear of the field. Considering the pressure he was under, as defending champion, he had gone out in 40 and stood just three over fours on the 13th tee. A huge gallery scurried over to hopefully witness the first round ever under eighty in the championship, but the last six holes took their toll, as they had done from time immemorial! A second round of 88 maintained his lead, and Willie Fernie was runner-up with a pack of four St Andreans one shot behind him.

Robt . Ferguson.

Ferguson suffered poor health from the mid-1880s and went back to caddying, and despite failing eyesight, he "worked the bag" for a further thirty-seven years.

An elevated view of the 2nd from the green to tee - sweeping ridges shadowed by the late evening sun

3rd

"Cartgate out"

397 yard par 4

The 1888 and '91 Opens

Hole #3
"Cartgate Out"

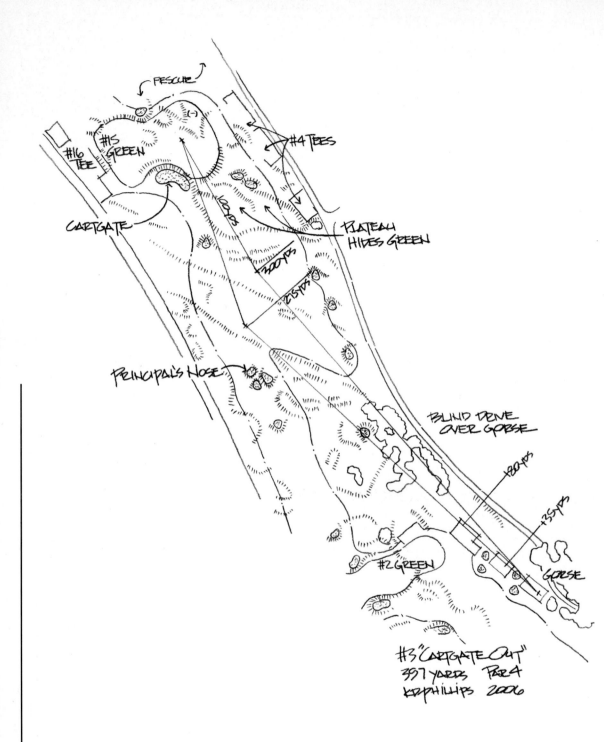

This hole is accommodating to a long drive played down the right side of this fairway shared with the 16th hole. Because the drive plays blind over the gorse bushes, it takes a combination of course knowledge, faith in one's caddies and trust in one's swing to execute properly. The faint-of-heart are tempted to favour the left off the tee, but the contours around the green favour a second shot from the right, as approaches arriving to the green from the left are easily deflected to the front right approach area. A large plateau that hides the green from view extends some 70 yards from the front of the green. This grand land-form not only adds to the complexity and mystery of the approach, but contains the large "Cartgate" bunker which is eager to gather up shots short and left of the green.

Architectural Sketch & Comments by Kyle Phillips

An aerial view of the 3rd, running alongside the white shale path Which splits the New Course from the Old Course, reveals all of the bunkers on the fairway and undulations around the green.

G reenkeepers manicure the expansive 3rd green and fairway in early-morning sunlight in preparation for the first day's play of the 2005 Open Championship. To the right, in shade, is Cartgate bunker.

After Bob Martin's second win at St Andrews in 1885, The Open returned again in 1888 when Jack Burns, representing an English club in Warwickshire, (but a born and bred St Andrean), was the unexpected winner. In this illustration Burns is proudly wearing his championship medal.

Described as "a strapping young fellow", Burns had mastered the blustery conditions on the day with rounds of 86 and 85, and just pipped Ben Sayers from North Berwick and one of the St Andrews Anderson brothers by a shot, after a three-way tie had wrongly been declared before the cards were checked! Hardly any prize money had been raised by the R & A membership, as the gentlemen had left the town on hearing that the championship, for some reason, had been postponed by a week. Jack Burns received £8.00 with meagre pickings left for the rest of the field!

On the course, Burns used to brag that he had not been off the line for years! (He had moved back to St Andrews and worked on the railway for 20 years!) He is seen here in later life, sitting on a railing by the 18th green, emery papering (taking the rust off) a club, one of the caddie's duties after carrying for his gentleman.

ST ANDREWS CADDIES

When golf bags were introduced prior to the 1888 Open at St Andrews, the local caddies feared that they would become redundant! They needn't have worried, for the bond between the caddie and "his man" was, and still is, an integral part of the game. In recent times "Tip" Anderson, and his father before him, were the best known of the St Andrews caddies. Sadly "Tip" died in 2004 and I was asked to present a tribute to him at his funeral. In a packed town church, it finished with a message from Arnold Palmer, which in its simplicity spoke volumes about the relationship – it just said "goodbye old friend".

The original "big three" of Robertson, Park and Morris were all recognised caddies in the 1850s, relying on this work to supplement their income. J. O. Fairlie (whom Morris caddied for twenty years) wrote on behalf of Prestwick to six other clubs in 1860 inviting them to send a representative to play in what was to be the first Open championship. He said, "It is desirable that the player be known as a respectable caddie". Tom Morris, as "keeper of the green" on the Old Course, was among other things, in charge of the caddies. On his list of seventeen regulars in 1883, four of them were past Open winners.

"Tip" Anderson – Arnold Palmer's caddie for thirty-five years in Britain. From 1960 they teamed up for all the Opens, Ryder Cups and match-play tournaments!

A St Andrews caddie, David Corstorphine, circa 1905 – still carrying the clubs under his arm, even with the new-fangled golf bag …… old habits die hard!

In the beginning, sand was taken from the hole, and from one club-length away the ball mounted up and swiped down the next fairway! Later, sand would be provided in a tee box, or from a caddie's pocket!!

Golf bags introduced at the R & A Autumn Meeting in 1888

Below is a line-up of registered caddies in front of the Clubhouse in 1892. They were all local fisher folk who relied on finding work on the links during the summer months. The tall one in the centre is my great-grandfather, Willie Joy. They were all characters with their own distinctive nicknames, such as "Treacle," "Skipper", "Trap Door", "Pint Size", "Stumpie Eye", "Wiggy" and "Sodger". One of them, Donal Blue, had postcards made of himself in makeshift Highland dress and size- twelve boots, sold on as a souvenir from St Andrews!

"THE LADYHEAD"

The cathedral end of North Street was the fishermen's quarters, known as "The Ladyhead". This photograph is one of the earliest ever taken in 1842. From this densely-populated (but small) area, all the caddies and five past Open champions were bred! Out on the street and in the doorways, hand lines were baited with mussels (from the Eden estuary) and fish were gutted by the womenfolk as their husbands and sons touted for work on the Old Course after an early-morning catch. The photograph opposite shows the same doorway today.

The whole area surrounding the caddies'/fishermen's quarters in the old part of town is atmospheric. There was a saying that originated from here, that when someone was uncomfortable, it was because they had left the shadow of the square tower (of the cathedral)!

The photograph is of the St Andrews Preservation Trust Museum, in the heart of the "Ladyhead". It houses photographs of the daily comings and goings of the fisherfolk up to the turn of the century (1900) and gives a real insight into how hard it was for them to make a living. The Trust was set up in 1937 "to preserve, for the benefit of the public, the amenities and historic character of the city and Royal Burgh of St Andrews".

THE
STARTERS
BOX

This converted Victorian bathing hut, normally used by ladies "dipping" on the West Sands, was wheeled out onto the 1st tee of the Old Course every morning from about 1890 to 1925.

In 1891 St Andrews born-and-bred professionals would come to the fore again on their home course – but for the last time! Only Bob Ferguson had broken their monopoly since 1873. Eight of the top ten in this championship were members of the St Andrews Golf Club, including the winner, Hugh Kirkaldy, and his brother Andrew, who beat Willie Fernie (also a club member, but representing Troon), in a play-off over one round the next day for runner-up. The St Andrews Club today has a champion's gallery in their main bar which boasts twenty-one Open wins, three US Open Champions, two British and one US Amateur Champion – and all before 1903!!

The winner in 1891, Hugh Kirkaldy, beat his brother by two shots with two rounds of eighty-three. The first was in heavy rain; the second, as the weather cleared in the afternoon, was the first winner's card without more than a five on it! He had nine straight fives all the way in on the back nine.

Hugh Kirkaldy was known as "The St Andrews Swing"; energetic and very full. It was similar to that of the 1995 winner John Daly (see page 175 for comparison). The one difference was that Kirkaldy, instead of watching the ball, followed the club head until it disappeared from sight on the backswing and waited for it to come down again!!

Unfortunately, Hugh, like so many great players before him, died young, after suffering from a severe bout of influenza just six years after his home win.

Hugh Kirkaldy with "The St Andrews Swing"

4th

"Ginger Beer"

480 yard par 4

End of an era and the emergence of
"The Triumvirate" in 1895

Hole #4 – "Ginger Beer"

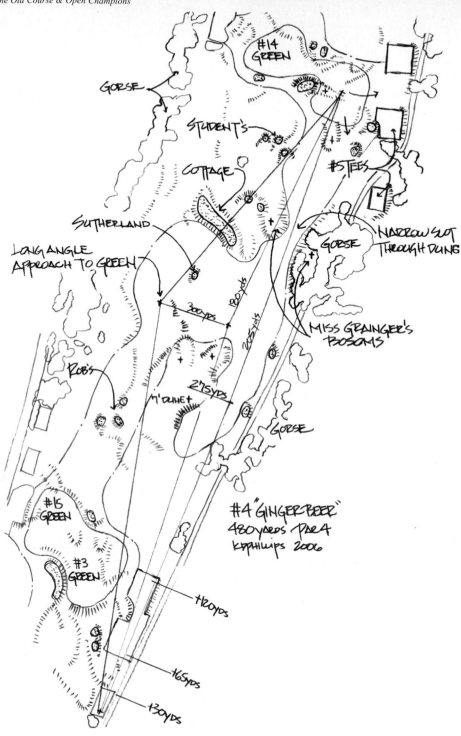

GORSE

#14 GREEN

STUDENT'S

COTTAGE

#5 TEES

SUTHERLAND

NARROW SLOT THROUGH DUNE

LONG ANGLE APPROACH TO GREEN

GORSE

300 yds

180 yds

205 yds

MISS GRAINGER'S BOSOMS

ROB'S

4' DUNE

275 yds

GORSE

#15 GREEN

#3 GREEN

#4 "GINGER BEER"
480 yards PAR 4
K.D. Phillips 2006

170 yds

165 yds

130 yds

This hole, the longest par 4 at the Old Course, requires an extremely long and accurate drive between the dunes on the left and the gorse on the right. Few are able to carry far enough to reach the wide part of the fairway. The preferred line of play down the right side of the fairway is very thin, if one has hopes of catching a glimpse of the approach and flag between the two dunes short of the green known as Miss Grainger's Bosoms. Drives that are played on a line into the 15th fairway will be faced with the most difficult of second shots, as the green is guarded by a strong ridge that sweeps approach shots to the right, and a deep bunker on the left.

Architectural Sketch & Comments by Kyle Phillips

The landing area is not visible from the 4th tee but lies between the gorse and bunkers on the right and the rough grassed ridge on the left. The tee shot requires accuracy and length to have any chance of attacking the flag.

The large bunker beside the 4th green adds to the challenge of a long approach shot into this par 4.

The 4th hole, "Ginger Beer" was so named for providing refreshments! A wicker-work basket on wheels was pushed out onto the course and supplied milk, half lemons, golf balls and ginger beer. This illustration shows Tom Morris partaking of a glass, with his caddie "Daw" Anderson slicing a lemon.

BY THE TIME THE OPEN RETURNED TO ST ANDREWS, IN 1895,

After Kirkaldy's win on the Old Course in 1891, Prestwick wrote to the other two clubs involved in hosting the Championship calling a meeting to discuss extending the competition to England. They suggested including the greens of Royal Liverpool, Hoylake, and St George's at Sandwich.

The Honourable Company of Edinburgh Golfers, who were responsible for running the Musselburgh Open, had already acquired ground and commissioned Tom Morris to lay out the Muirfield course, at Gullane, as a new venue. The Musselborough public were up in arms over this rather clumsy boot into touch, but its nine-hole-course had become congested and run-down.

And so it was the next year that the eighteen-hole course "Muirfield" hosted the Open. Despite the course being criticised by some professionals as "a bit short and waterlogged in places", the tournament was a success. It was successful because the format was changed. Four rounds were played over two days, with an entry fee of ten shillings introduced to deter the "no-hopers" from playing. For example, Willie Steele, an amateur representing Bruntsfield

MANY QUITE DRAMATIC CHANGES HAD TAKEN PLACE

in the first Open, made up the numbers and went round three times, on the twelve-hole course at Prestwick, in sixteen over sixes!

The three host clubs met the following year (1893), and stated that they would "place the competition on a basis more commensurate with its importance than had hitherto existed." The delegates decided that if Sandwich and Hoylake were to be involved, each of the five clubs contribute £15 towards prize money and that at least £100 (which they managed to raise at Muirfield) should be provided. The winner to receive £30 plus £10 for a gold medal, £20 for the runner-up, and the rest appropriately paid out down to £1 for twelfth place!

All was agreed and 1894 saw the first Open to be played in England and at a more civilised time of the year – June. No longer would pressure be put on the members, of the host club, to dig into their pockets to provide the last of "the entertainment" during the Autumn Meeting. The Open would now be able to stand up for itself, as the game attracted more and more attention, and courses and would-be-champions emerged throughout the length and breadth of the British Isles.

If St Andrews-born Willie Auchterlonie (left) had been told that, after his win at Prestwick in 1893, there would not be another home-based Scot win The Open for one hundred and six years, he would probably just have laughed! His fellow Scottish professionals would have been equally incredulous at such a statement, they were so dominant at that point. Only a great English Amateur Champion, Mr John Ball, representing Royal Liverpool, had managed to win in 1890 at Prestwick. Huge changes were afoot until Paul Lawrie (above) eventually broke the taboo at Carnoustie in 1999.

J. H. Taylor, double winner at St Andrews with back-to-back wins in 1895 and 1900.

After J.H. Taylor's heroic victory in 1895, he successfully defended his St Andrews title when The Open returned to the Old Course five years later. He demolished the field by eight shots, with Harry Vardon his nearest rival. His last round, witnessed by a huge crowd, was to be a new Championship record score of seventy-five. That year, and the next, the "Triumvirate" finished first, second and third! Taylor was a great ambassador for his fellow professionals and was instrumental in setting up the Professional Golf Association. In his fifties he was still in contention in the 1922 Open. He became Captain of the Ryder Cup Team in 1933 – and an Honorary member of the R & A in 1950, and lived an active life up until his ninety-second year when he died in 1963.

After J.H. Taylor won the first Open played in England on the Sandwich course in 1894, he came up the following year to St Andrews in a blaze of glory to defend his title against the Scots. Golf was attracting "media attention" with the first two golf magazines established and published on a regular basis. The national and local press were popularising the great challenge matches, competitions and characters prominent in the game.

Taylor did not let himself or his country down, and won convincingly on the Old Course by four shots from up-and-coming local professional Sandy Herd. Trailing the Scot by three going into the final round, J.H. battled his way round in a strong wind and shot 78, when more than half the field failed to break 90.

With a great chance to win three in a row, Taylor stumbled when fellow Englishman Harry Vardon beat him in a play-off at Muirfield. This heralded the start of an era dominated by Vardon, Taylor and Scotsman James Braid. Amongst them they won sixteen Opens from 1894 to 1914, prior to the outbreak of the Great War which caused the Championship to be abandoned for five years. Vardon still holds the record of six wins although, but for "the rub of the green", Taylor could well have matched or overtaken him, having won five times and been runner-up on no fewer than six occasions.

Willie Park Jnr, son of the first Open champion and a winner in his own right (1887 and 1889). Although playing well, he decided not to enter the 1895 Open through pressure of work – designing courses!

THE TRIUMVIRATE

With sixteen wins in the Open Championship
between them from 1894 – 1914

Harry Vardon	1896, '98, '99, 1903, '11, '14
J. H. Taylor	1894, '95, 1900, '09, '13
James Braid	1901, '05, '06, '08, '10

HARRY VARDON

The 1905 winner, James Braid, although representing an English club – Walton Heath, was a popular local winner for he was born and brought up in Elie, just twelve miles down the coast from St Andrews. As a nine-year-old boy he had followed Jamie Anderson around the Old Course when he won the 1879 Open. After Anderson looked at the young Braid's swing he was told that he too might be an Open Champion at St Andrews one day. In the year that Anderson died that mission was accomplished, with great panache.

Braid was a tall man who hit the ball prodigious distances off the tee. As the first man to break 70 in The Open (at Sandwich in 1904) he was expected to break records on the Old Course with the introduction of the new "bounding ball". Lengthening of the tees, and the addition of

J. H. TAYLOR

JAMES BRAID

pot bunkers, were put in place to protect the course from the extra yards gained with the new rubber-cored Haskell ball. It was yet another chapter in the evolution of the Old Course and its constant battle to protect itself against technology without compromising its character and tradition. As had often been the case, adverse weather conditions were the great protector of the course, and Braid's winning score was in fact nine shots behind Taylor's emphatic win with the old gutty ball in 1900.

THE SCOTS VERSUS THE ENGLISH!

A great rivalry between the Scots and English developed with ten-a-side matches played regularly on various greens throughout the land. Great crowd pleasers around the turn of the century were matches billed "Scotland versus England" when Vardon and Taylor took on Braid and Herd. They attracted large partisan galleries wherever and whenever they played. Braid was to win five Opens from 1901 to 1910 and although Herd only won in 1902, he was always there, or thereabouts. More often than not the matches were close-run and dramatic confrontations with the highest standards in golf guaranteed.

James Braid and Sandy Herd, winner and runner-up in the 50th Anniversary Open, were partners in the Scotland versus England matches from 1900-14.

In the 50th Anniversary Open in 1910 there was much speculation as to which of "The Triumvirate" might win. At that time they all had four wins each to their name. Two hundred and ten competitors (only nine amateurs) entered with the top sixty going through to the second day. The first day's play had to be cancelled mid-afternoon when a thunderstorm engulfed the course. James Braid was eventually victorious with rounds of 76, 73, 74 and 76, beating his Scottish playing partner Sandy Herd by four shots.

Braid was carried aloft from the last green by an ecstatic crowd to be presented with the Claret Jug for a record fifth win. At the presentation ceremony, Braid, after picking up his prize money of £50.00, gave his winner's medal to the R & A to show permanently in their Clubhouse as a gesture and acknowledgement of their involvement in running the 50th Anniversary Championship.

THE NEW COURSE

The New Course was opened officially the day after the conclusion of the 1895 Open. The top twenty played a round to set the course record, bearing in mind that J. H. Taylor had two 78s on his way to winning the championship on the Old – 85 was the best they could do on the New. It was considered "More treacherous – with frightening hazards" than the Championship Course itself. Sixty years later Frank Jowle, a little-known English Professional, caused a sensation qualifying on the New Course in the 1955 Open by scoring 63 – it produced the fine headline "Cheek by Jowle!"

4th green

Tom Morris had originally laid out the New Course with a budget of just under £100.00 per hole. It is the only one, of all the courses he designed, that still has its greens in their original positions today. The Royal and Ancient paid for its construction to alleviate pressure on the number of rounds played on the Old Course. They still maintain rights today, and play many of their Spring and Autumn competitions on it.

From 1921 the New Course was used for qualifying for the Open until 1970 and it is still one of the most testing and under-rated links courses in the country.

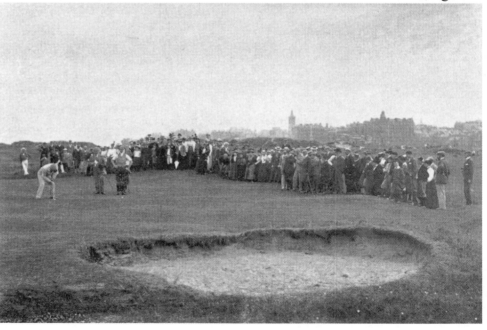

1st green on the New Course 1895

The New Course 17th, a long par 3, beside the 1st green on the Jubilee Course.

The par 3 13th green is protected by two deep bunkers on either side of a steep slope guarding the flag. Behind is the 10th green looking down its naturally shaped fairway and to the left of that is the 11th tee to green (in the distance).

almer's new caddie, local man "Tip" Anderson, was anxious that he hadn't had a practice round on the New Course before the 1960 Championship began. Palmer's response was that if "Tip" (off a three handicap) had played it often enough – why should he bother! It was the start of a long and fruitful partnership with the winning of the next two Championships at Birkdale and Troon.

The evergreen Gene Sarazen led the qualifying on the Old and the New during the Centenary Open, aged fifty-eight – twenty-eight years after having won at Sandwich. Up until the late 50s it had been both physically and mentally tiring playing two qualifying and four regular rounds in three days. At that time they teed off Tuesday, Wednesday and Thursday, which allowed time for the Club Professionals to get back and sort out their members' tee times for the weekend!

Arnold Palmer playing on the New Course during qualifying for the Centenary Open in 1960.

5th

"Hole O' Cross Out"

568 yard par 5

Farewell to Old Tom

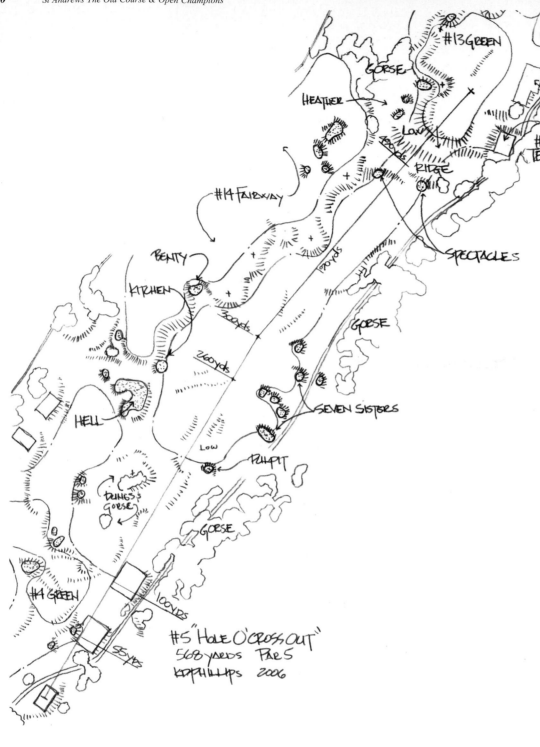

Hole #5
"Hole O'Cross Out"

Unlike the predictable bunkering of American-style courses today, the drive on the 5th is an example of how the Old Course is strewn with hidden revetted bunkers that may appear to some to have no purpose, at least not until an inadvertent shot is played into one of them.

The preferred drive down the left should avoid the "Seven Sister" and "Pulpit" that are scattered down the right side of the fairway. However, a drive played too far left leaves a second shot blinded by the long high dune that runs parallel down the left. A thrilling second shot awaits, requiring a carry over the large dune ridge containing the "Spectacles" and a deep swale in front of the green. Those who choose to lay-up short of the dune ridge face a blind third shot to this, the world's largest green.

Architectural Sketch & Comments by Kyle Phillips

An aerial view of the 5th, hugging the right-hand footpath. To the bottom left are the "Seven Sisters" bunkers (see over), hidden from the tee, with the 5th and 13th double green top right.

THE "SEVEN SISTERS"

This group of seven revetted bunkers, ready to catch any drive right of the 5th fairway, was structured by Tom Morris when money was made available to shape many of the natural hazards in 1887. The inset picture shows how the ground lay before this project began.

A hard frost may delay play on a winter's day but heavy snow lying for any length of time is a rarity.

This late afternoon picture of the 5th and 13th greens, with a deep covering of snow, on a very cold

January day halted play for seven days, but provided a winter wonderland rarely seen on these links.

DOUBLE GREENS

To ease congestion in the mid 1850s the greens were extended to allow two flags on seven of the holes and help speed-up play. Up until that point, inward players had the right of way to the flag simply by playing the same nine holes back towards the town. When more ground running parallel to the original course was acquired in 1870 the eighteen-hole Old Course that we recognise today was adapted to suit its already established long greens. The double greens are a major feature of the course, and none more talked about in the world of golf than the shared 5th and 13th. The 5th green was described as far back as 1857 as "the truest and finest in the country". It can claim some of the longest putts ever struck in the history of the game! Kyle Phillips' sketch of the 11th and 7th greens (next page) show a yardage of 110 from top to bottom!

It is a quirky fact that the double greens all add up to the number eighteen (2nd with 16th and so on) and that only four greens on the Old Course stand alone.

Above: The 5th and 13th double green surrounded by gorse in bloom.

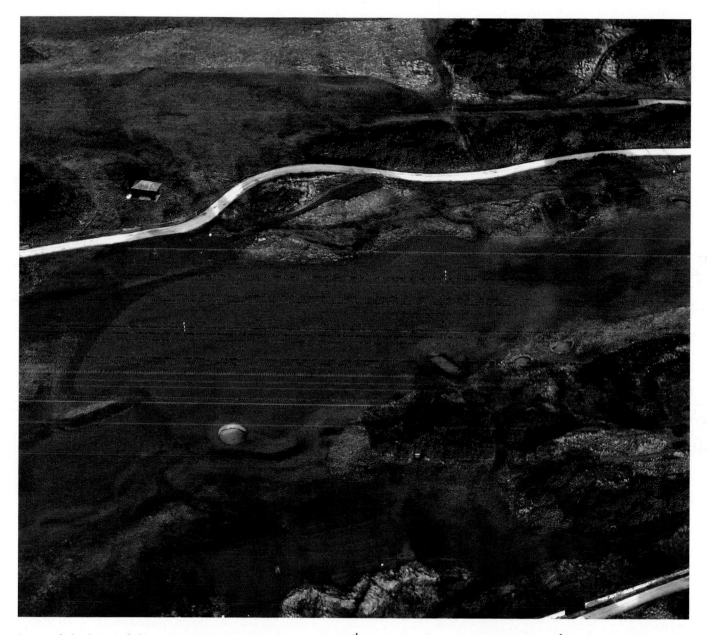

An aerial view of the enormous double–green, the 5th playing from the right and 13th playing from the left.

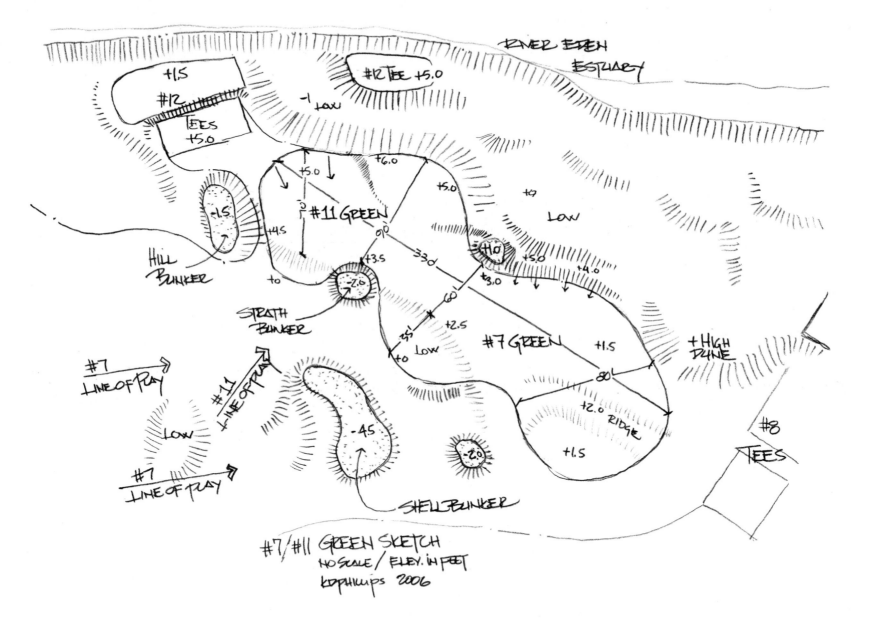

Sketch of the interesting 7th and 11th double green, the only hole where golfers play across each other.

See also picture on page 141.

FAREWELL TO "OLD TOM" 1821-1908

Old Tom watched Braid win at St Andrews in 1905, but died just two years before the 50th anniversary of the Open was hosted on "his course"! A bust of Tom Morris was placed under the clock on the front of the R & A clubhouse in that anniversary year, looking out over the home hole re-named "Tom Morris" after his retiral. His portrait painted by a prominent member of the club, Sir George Reid, hangs above the fireplace in the main room of the Clubhouse today.

THE JUBILEE COURSE

The Jubilee, opened during Queen Victoria's Diamond Jubilee in 1897, was a twelve-hole course intending to cater for the novice or lady golfer. Tom Morris was given a budget of £12.00 per hole to lay out a short course to alleviate the pressure of play during the summer months, but it was soon converted to a full eighteen-hole course. Through the years eminent course designers H.S. Colt and Donald Steel have had a hand in re-shaping what is now considered by locals to be the most difficult of all the home courses to score on from medal tees.

The approach view to the par 5 6th green.

Out on the course the flag sits near the front of the green on the testing par 5 12th hole in autumnal light.

THE EDEN COURSE

In 1914 the course opened – again to absorb the ever-increasing demand for more golf on the links of St Andrews. Harry Colt was sought after and eventually agreed to lay out this new course. He was probably the most underrated golf course architect in his day. Colt is often talked about by his fellow architects today as one of the true geniuses of golf course design.

While the Eden was under construction, Colt was in partnership with Alistair Mackenzie and also working on two courses in the States (one of them with Donald Ross), one in Canada and another in England that year. By 1920, the Eden hosted its own tournament which became a major match-play competition on the Scottish circuit. The course was re-vamped in 1989 but retains some of its old charm. It still meanders in part around the Eden Estuary (as below on the 4th hole).

The Eden Estuary skirts the right side of the 4th fairway.

The Eden course still retains its original character with its whins, wispy grass and undulations intact. This photograph shows a wayward approach to the 7th green.

THE STRATHTYRUM COURSE

In 1993 another short eighteen hole course was constructed to provide an easier test of golf than its four big brothers. More ground had to be acquired by the Links Trust and the Cheapes family duly obliged by giving up part of the old Strathtyrum Estate. The 17th century palace or mansion house of Archbishop Sharpe lies hidden away behind an avenue of trees, within the grounds. This aerial picture shows the most westerly point of the estuary where the Eden and Strathtyrum courses run side by side.

6th

"Heathery Out"

412 yard par 4

The Open returned to the Old Course after the Great
War and heralded "An American Invasion"
of the Championship for thirteen years.

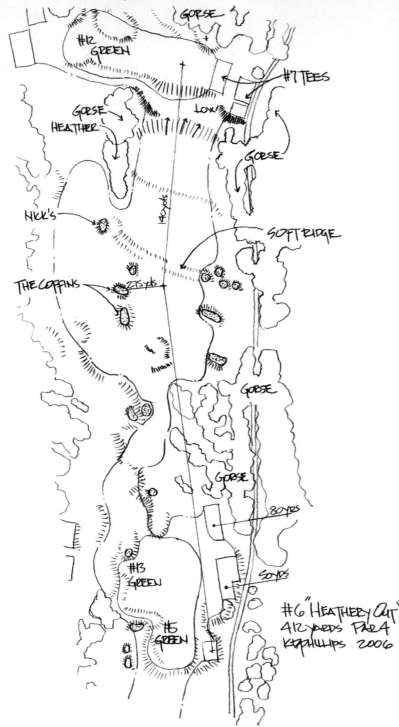

Hole # 6

"Heathery Out"

While gorse bushes once again obscure the tee shot on this hole, this drive unlike many others at the Old Course offers no real alternate line of play. Use of the adjacent 13th fairway is denied by "The Coffins" and "Nick's" to the left of the landing area and the right side of the fairway is guarded by a series of six bunkers. A good drive will set up a short approach and birdie opportunity to this bunkerless green. Beware, however, that the front of the green spills off sharply, pulling weak approaches back down into the deep tightly- mown blind hollow short of the green, making for delicate recovery shots back up to the pin.

Opposite: Aerial view of the 6th, bordered on the right by the white shale path and New Course.

Architectural Sketch & Comments by Kyle Phillips

A blind tee shot over the heather-covered ridge, avoiding gorse and bunkers to the right, and "The Coffins" to the left.

When the Championship returned to St Andrews after the Great War, the R & A had taken over the entire responsibility of The Open and Amateur tournaments. The 1921 Open was eventful with the arrival of "The Boy Wonder" Bobby Jones, which heralded the start of the American invasion. Jock Hutchison, after a two round play-off against Mr Roger Wethered, lifted the Claret Jug. It was very much a head-to-head between the experienced pro and the sporting amateur. Wethered, representing the R & A, was decisively beaten by nine shots – but accepted defeat graciously!

Hutchison was declared the first American winner, even though he was a born-and-bred St Andrean! He had emigrated six years before and taken up US citizenship. The young Bobby Jones had created a stir when, on his third round, he struggled to the turn in 46 – double bogeyed the 10th, and after four stabs in "Hill" Bunker by the 11th green, he "retired".

Hutchison deserved his win having led the qualifying and all four rounds of the Championship – although J.H. Taylor complained that he bought his win out of a shop – this was a reference to Hutchison's new "ribbed" irons.

Jock Hutchison lining up an approach shot with one of his controversial ribbed irons – declared illegal by the Rules Committee one week after he had won the Open with them!

THE AMERICAN INVASION

From 1921 to 1933 the Open produced a long line of American winners – Walter Hagen and Bobby Jones won seven between them in nine years, as well as a string of US Open titles. Many would sail over from New York for the summer month of the Open and supplemented their income by playing exhibition matches throughout the country to justify the expensive trip. The flamboyant Walter Hagen was always the star attraction at such events, but had a great supporting cast in Sarazen, Farrel, Diegel, Barnes and MacDonald-Smith. As for the Open itself, £225.00 was the total prize money to be shared out, with the winner receiving £100.00.

Englishman Arthur Havers was the only man in 1923 to interrupt the run of American Open victories. After Jones retired, having achieved "The Grand Slam" of golf in 1930, Tommy Armour, Gene Sarazen, then Densmore Shute won the next three, representing the US.

Jim Barnes was the first and last American winner at Prestwick in 1925! It was to be the last of twenty-five Opens hosted by Prestwick after crowds had severely disrupted play. Barnes was in fact English, who, like Hutchison had emigrated to the USA earlier.

Popular American, Walter Hagen, holds the Claret Jug and his medal after his first of four wins in the 1920s – 1922 and '28 at Sandwich, '24 at Hoylake and '29 at Muirfield.

When Mr Robert Tyre "Bobby" Jones came back to St Andrews it was to practice and play in the Walker Cup in 1926. He took time to study the Old Course – "you have to study it," he said, "and the more you study the more you learn; the more you learn the more you study it".

As the then-current Open Champion, having won in Lytham the previous year, he successfully defended his title in 1927 with style. He opened up with a record breaking 68 in the first round, holing putts of all shapes and sizes! The great amateur was in complete control of his game apart from driving into "Cheape's" Bunker off

the 2nd tee, three times out of the four rounds. What a following he had, and what a hugely popular win by the twenty-five year old who had already achieved so much in the game. Having quickly erased the memory of his first Open in 1921, Jones only came over and played in three more Championships, and won them all – the last being at Hoylake in his Grand Slam year of 1930.

Above: Bobby Jones after his win at St Andrews in 1927.

Left: Jock Hutchison taking the Open Trophy back with him to the States for the first time in 1921.

ST ANDREWS AND THE FIRST LEG
OF THE GRAND SLAM

Bobby Jones said "The most important achievement of my life was winning the first leg of the Grand Slam- the British Amateur Championship at St Andrews in 1930".

He was particularly nervous about the week ahead as all the rounds up to the final were just over 18 holes, playing two matches a day. In the third round the great confrontation took place between himself and Cyril Tolley, the defending Champion. With a strong wind blowing, in a tense and titanic struggle, Tolley had a twelve-foot putt on the last green to win, and put paid to the idea of the Grand Slam.

He missed and Jones won with a stymie on the 19th green. "I was neither exultant or elated – just very, very tired at the end of it," said Jones. Having reached the final he was confident of beating Roger Wethered over two rounds. The R & A's main man, Wethered, had had a gruelling draw on the way to squaring up with Jones and was jaded. It was thought that Wethered was just too charming on the course and lacked that hard streak needed to disturb Jones. Such was the case, and after being five up by the Road Hole in the morning and playing consistently thereafter, Jones won comfortably 6 and 5. His score recorded over the 31 holes were twenty-three 4^S, five 3^S and three 5^S.

Jones with the Grand Slam trophies – the British and American Amateur and Open Championships.

7th

"High Out"

390 yard par 4

The 1933 Open – and a play-off!

Hole #7 – "High Out"

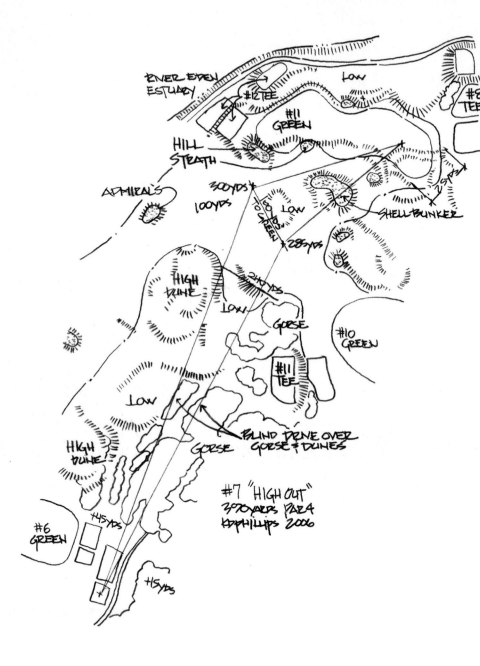

The blind drive on this first crossing hole requires a long carry over dunes and gorse in order to reach this wide fairway. The dominant feature of the fairway is a strong depression 100 yards from green along the play line. Arrival to the landing area provides a welcome full view of this double green that plays across the play line of the par 3 11th hole. The approach is more difficult than it first appears and requires the proper combination of distance and direction, lest the strong contours of the green quickly pull the less than perfect approach shots off the green to the right.

Be assured if the Old Course were being designed today, the 7th hole would play to the 11th green and the 11th hole would play to the 7th green in order to 'avoid any conflict' of play, thus 'avoiding' one of the most magical moments of the Old Course.

Architectural Sketch & Comments by Kyle Phillips

The approach view to the 7th green, featuring "Shell" bunker.

SHELL BUNKER AND 7th GREEN

Shell is the second-biggest bunker on the course after "Hell"! It was originally filled with barrow loads of crushed shells collected from the Eden Estuary behind the green. This was the most practical way of maintaining such a large bunker in the 1850s. The front facing of it today is well above head height.

Scottish links courses, all the way round the east coast, have always been threatened by erosion. With the relentless pounding of winter North Sea breakers sucking away protective dunes nearest the tide line, some of our oldest traditional holes lie vulnerable.

When Tom Morris took on the job of "keeper of the green" in 1864, he feared that the old 7th green might disappear completely when he went out to inspect it at times. To combat this he sent to Holland for "sea-lyme grass" which retained the sand around its wiry roots, and in time reclaimed a good area of ground.

In the 1933 Open as strong a field as would be seen until the '64 Open assembled on the Old Course for its Championship. The Ryder Cup Teams of both America and Great Britain played. Densmore Shute, in his first appearance in The Open, was the surprise winner as the big named players Sarazen, Diegel, Cotton and Mitchell all fell away in the final round. Shute had been the most consistent player that week but never broke par in qualifying, in the four Championship rounds or even in the play-off against long-hitting Craig Wood. Four rounds of par 73 (the 17th was still a par 5 at that time) and two play-off rounds of 75 and 74 were good enough to win.

Walter Hagen, who started with a record equalling 68 followed by a 72, had a miserable time on the last two rounds, dropping fifteen shots to par. The fairways were parched brown that year and the ball seemed to roll forever – but with an unpredictable bounce many of the favoured players came to grief when least expected.

Densmore Shute, the 1933 Open Champion.

8th

"Short"

175 yard par 3

The Championship before and
after the war, 1939 and 1946.

Hole # 8 – "Short"

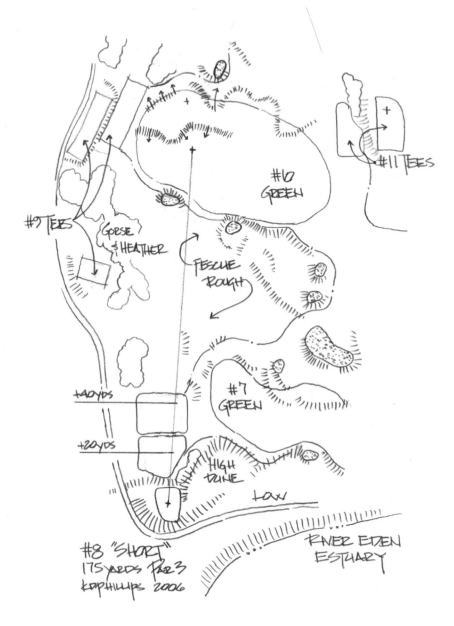

#11 TEES

#10 GREEN

#9 TEES

GORSE & HEATHER

FESCUE ROUGH

#7 GREEN

+40 YDS

+20 YDS

HIGH DUNE

LOW

RIVER EDEN ESTUARY

#8 "SHORT"
175 yards Par 3
KDPHILLIPS 2006

Links golf is typically associated with the ability to play running shots in the wind, but this 3 par hole is a break from that tradition. Instead of a lead-in fairway, this green is completely absent of fairway. It is fronted by an abundance of heather and fescue, as well as a small hidden pot bunker. Even when playing down wind there is ample green depth to carry the rough and hold the short approach.

Architectural Sketch & Comments by Kyle Phillips

The 8th tee to green view.

In the Open of 1933 the course was running hard and fast. Craig Wood, the big-hitting American, ended up in the left hand "Spectacle" bunker off the 5th tee. From today's Championship tee that would measure around 490 yards; - though where he drove from is debatable, one thing is certain: that the carry on the flight of the ball would have been less than the distance achieved by the bounce and roll when it hit the fairway – especially if the shape of the shot had a draw on it.

For the 1939 Open the 5th and 14th tees were lengthened to allow players room to swing! There had always been congestion around the par 5's with spectators crowding in on them for a better view. Stewards or marshals, made up of volunteers from the town, were introduced. They donned white coats and carried long bamboo poles which held horizontally created a barrier of sorts!

Craig Wood in 1933, hitting the longest drive ever recorded on the Old.

Englishman Dick Burton, after his win in 1939, had to wait a further seven years, with the outbreak of war, to defend his championship. Maybe the pressure got to him for he stood on the first tee in 1946 and carved his drive out of bounds! In 1939 around 5,000 spectators a day paid to watch the play. Most followed just two matches; that of Henry Cotton – who had stopped the American monopoly of the Championship by winning at Sandwich in 1934 and again at Carnoustie in 1937. The other Crowd-puller was a talented young South African, Bobby Locke, who would eventually win his fourth Open in 1957 at St Andrews. It was worrying that hardly any of the established players from the States thought it worthwhile to make the long journey across the pond to compete. Only Shute and Sarazen, as past winners, entered. Neither made the cut which was drastically reduced to just 34 competitors. Johnny Bulla, representing Chicago, was the lone American who played well and finished runner-up just two shots behind Burton.

Bobby Locke had stood at six under 4s on the new 14th tee on the first round, but into the wind could not carry " The Beardies". Having extracted himself from one group of three bunkers, his next landed in "Hell", and eventually a good putt holed got him an eight!

The winner, Dick Burton, was regarded at that time as the longest driver in British Professional golf.

The firm favourite, Henry Cotton, just failed to get fired up with rounds of 74, 72, 76 and 76 – finishing eight shots behind the winner.

Old Pros Willie Auchterlonie (winner in 1893) and, to his right, Sandy Herd (winner in 1902) were still competing in the '39 Open.

"SLAMMIN SAM" SNEAD

Joint runner-up Bobby Locke looks on as Snead receives the trophy.

S am Snead arrived just two days before the start of the 1946 Open. He seemed almost reluctant to be there and disturbed many with his comments. His first reaction to the course as his train skirted the 15th and 16th was "an old abandoned kind of place this". On playing the Old for the first time he described its big double greens as "absurd".

The tournament got under way and out of 268 entries, 100 qualified and Henry Cotton with two 70's led Snead by a shot at the half way stage. Welshman Da Rees broke Bobby Jones' long standing record with a 67 in the second round. Snead eventually pulled away from the field with relentlessly long driving, finding the par four 9th, 10th and 12th greens, round "The Loop", off the tee. His fellow American Johnny Bulla was runner-up again in an Open at St Andrews, tying with Bobby Locke. Despite his disparaging remarks about the Old Course and comments like, "whenever you leave the USA, boy, you're just camping out", he was a hugely popular winner. Snead endeared himself to everyone when fifty-four years after his victory, he returned and tap-danced his way across the Swilken Bridge when playing in the "The Parade of Champions" on the eve of the Millennium Open.

Sam Snead 1946

Ben Hogan on his only trip across to play in the Open, won at Carnoustie in 1953.

9th

"End"

352 yard par 4

Australian and South African wins in the '50s

Hole #9 – "End"

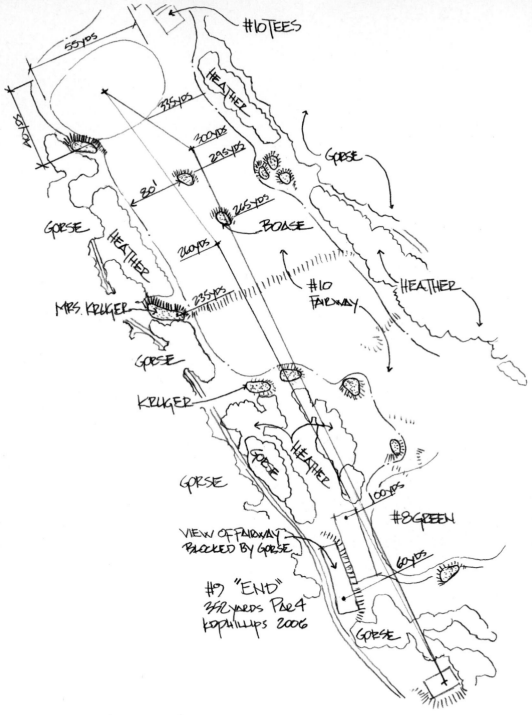

With the advance of technology, this par 4 hole offers little resistance to the professional player. The two central fairway bunkers and left green side bunkers are small and are non-gathering, thus long players fearlessly blast a drive towards the right half of the green. On the other hand, the original strategy of the centre bunkers are still in play for most amateurs and require real consideration from the tee.

Just when one is starting to believe that this course comprises of a collection of the most interesting greens in golf, the 9th green turns up! One is likely to consider that the real green must have been stolen, or that the putting surface is simply a tightly mown extension of the flat fairway. While the latter is true, this is just another example of how the Old Course knows no rules.

Architectural Sketch & Comments by Kyle Phillips

The view from the semi-blind 9th tee.

Australian Peter Thomson won by a shot from his main adversary throughout that decade, Bobby Locke, at St Andrews in 1955. Wins at Birkdale in '54 and Hoylake in '56 gave him three Open Championships in a row – last achieved by Bob Ferguson in 1882. Had Locke not pushed Thomson back into 2nd place in '57 he would have had five straight wins! The Open moved about after Snead won in 1946, and had been hosted on eight different venues before returning.

Thomson won with a record score of eleven under par. If anyone suggested his achievements in the 50s were against weak opposition, they were surely silenced at Birkdale when in 1965 he won for the fifth time, leaving Nicklaus and Palmer trailing in his wake nine and ten shots adrift!

After just one year away at Hoylake, the Open was back in St Andrews and Bobby Locke denied Thomson yet another win with rounds of '69, '72, '68 and '70. The Old Course suited Locke's style of play, which was to draw the ball away from trouble and let it run. He was a renowned putter and was in his element on its large greens.

This was the first year that the leaders went out last after the half way stage. This created a bit more drama as it was also the first year that the end of the Championship was shown on television although highlights had appeared on the screen in 1956.

South African winner, Bobby Locke, playing a "punched" shot into the 18th green in 1957.

The lean, willowy amateur of pre-war years was now a beefy, heavy-jowled four times winner of The Open Championship!

FREEDOM OF THE BURGH

In a packed Younger Graduation Hall in St Andrews on the 9th October 1958, Bobby Jones was made an honorary Burgess and granted the Freedom of the Burgh by Provost Leonard. It was an emotional night for all concerned. After being introduced as "a golfer of matchless skill and chivalrous spirit", Jones rose, and before his acceptance speech, stuffed his pre-prepared notes back into his pocket and talked from the heart. The last American to be to be acknowledged in such a way by the people of St Andrews was Benjamin Franklin, two hundred years before. Jones' closing remark was "if I could take out of my life everything but my experiences in St Andrews I would still have had a rich and full life". He left the building to the song "Will you no come back again" sung spontaneously by the whole assembled company.

10th

"Bobby Jones"

380 yard par 4

The Centenary Open.

Hole # 10
"Bobby Jones"

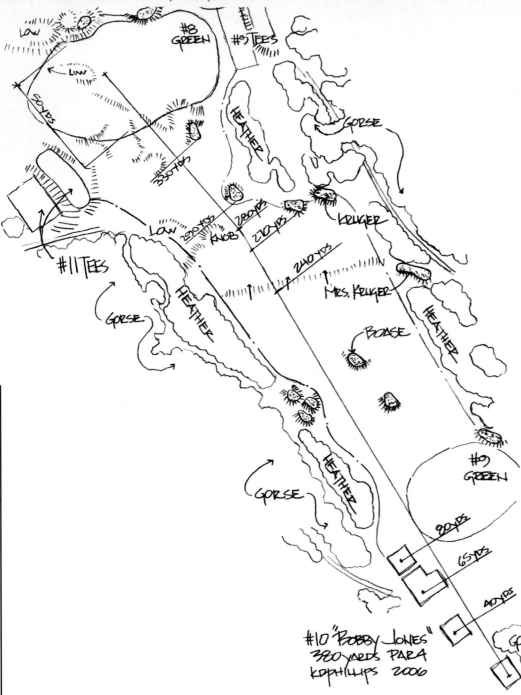

#10 "BOBBY JONES"
380 YARDS PAR 4
KDPHILLIPS 2006

The softly contoured fairway is visible from the tee with a strong line of gorse down the left rough. The fairway narrows with guarding bunkers approximately 100 yards from the green. The gently undulating green is over 50 yards deep, allowing for those seeking a birdie to attack the pin. When the winds are favourable, professionals will drive past the mound on the left and attempt to reach the green. This hole is named after the legendary 1927 Open winner who remained an amateur throughout his playing career.

Architectural Sketch & Comments by Kyle Phillips

With gorse and heather down the left side of the 10th fairway, this large pot bunker, short right of the green, frequently comes into play.

Arnold Palmer with local caddie "Tip" Anderson, driving from the 10th tee during the first round of the 1960 Open. The hole was the only one without a name until, on the recommendation of the Town Council, it was called "Bobby Jones". It was a final accolade from the town to their adopted American hero after his death in December 1971.

THE CENTENARY OPEN

The Old Course yet again created high drama in the 1960 Centenary Open. Surely no part of any course in the world has such a sense of theatre about it as its shared 1st and 18th fairways. The great box-office attraction was of course Arnold Palmer, fresh from his US Open win at Cherry Hills. His appearance injected new life into the Championship, and from that moment on with press and television coverage, the Open would attract worldwide attention.

Had Palmer holed his putts – had there not been a flash flood, which forced play to be suspended on the third day – he would surely have overhauled Nagle and walked away with the title.

Four shots behind the Australian with the last round to play, Palmer opened up with birdies on the first two holes, and his followers, who were to be christened "Arnie's Army", went wild. Nagle did well to withstand the pressure playing directly behind and matched Palmer's outward half of 34. The American attacked every hole but could not get a putt to drop until the 13th. Nagle dropped his first shot at the 15th and hung on to what he described as the most important and longest round of golf he had ever had to play in his life.

Robert De Vicenzo, an Argentinean representing Mexico at that time, opened up with two rounds of 67. This left Palmer trailing him by seven shots, but Vicenzo faltered and finished third equal. He would eventually win at Hoylake in 1967, which was a just reward in his nineteenth appearance at the Championship.

Kel Nagle, in the final pairing over the last two rounds, withstood the pressure of Palmer's charge. He manfully holed an eight footer on the 17th and matched Palmer's birdie on the last to win by one shot.

11th

"High In"

174 yard par 3

"Champagne Tony" in 1964.

Hole #11 – "High In"

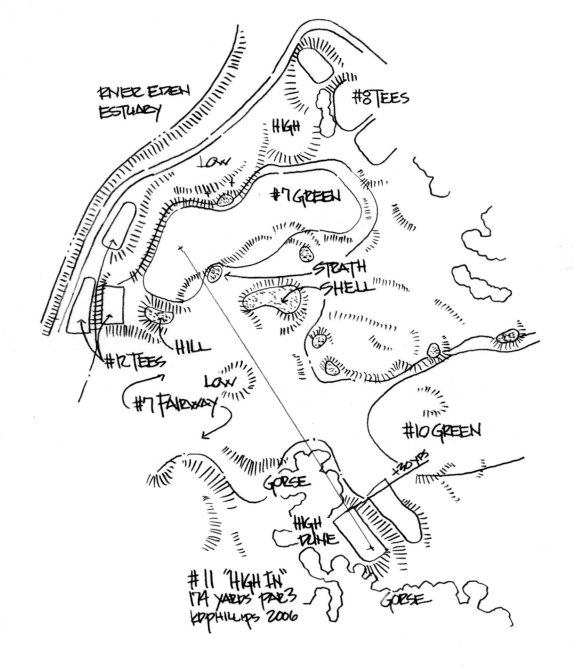

RIVER EDEN
ESTUARY

#8 TEES

HIGH

LOW

#7 GREEN

STRATH
SHELL

HILL

#12 TEES

LOW

#7 FAIRWAY

#10 GREEN

GORSE

+30 YDS

HIGH
DUNE

#11 "HIGH IN"
174 YARDS PAR 3
KDPHILLIPS 2006

GORSE

With a view of the Eden River Estuary in the backdrop, this, the second and final par 3 of the round, plays from an elevated tee. The green is guarded by the large "Shell" bunker short right of the green and "Hill" bunker on the left. But it is the "Strath" bunker that is the most intimidating of the three, with the favoured pin position just behind. The green is steeply contoured from back to front and set at a slight diagonal, requiring accurate distance and direction from the tee. Shots long will disappear into the long fescue of the deep hollow, leaving a very difficult recovery.

Architectural Sketch & Comments by Kyle Phillips

An aerial view of the 11th green (bottom left) to the tee (top right), also showing "Shell" bunker and the 10th green.

The 11th tee to green view.

"Hill" (to the left) and "Strath" (to the right) Bunkers flank the 11th green. "Hill" was named after the elevated carry needed up to where it guarded the old 7th green when the course was played in reverse. "Strath" was named after Allan

Strath who represented St Andrews in the first Open and won at Prestwick in 1865. He, as did his talented golfing brother David, died young.

[From a photo by J. Patrick & Sons, Edinburgh.

BUNKER AT 7TH (HIGH HOLE).

The above illustration shows "Hill" and "Strath" Bunkers in their natural state in 1870 – still formidable, but not as steep as the revetted "pits" you find yourself trapped in today. Bobby Jones (right) on his fourth attempt at extracting himself from "Hill" Bunker – his final shot of a disastrous round in the 1921 Open.

Lema, blown right of the fairway by a strong cross wind, plays out of the rough to the 3rd green. This was during the first day's play when exhibition tents were ripped by gale force winds, and Nicklaus described it as the worst weather conditions he had ever played in. Lema, avoiding the very worst of the weather, holed a forty-five foot putt on the last green to get round in 73.

It may have looked as if Tony Lema had just waltzed around the course with scores of 73, 68, 68 and 70 to beat Jack Nicklaus by five shots, but it wasn't quite that simple. With a nine-shot deficit "The Golden Bear", roared back with a 66 in the third round. During the last round, playing six holes ahead, Jack growled across at Lema on the shared 12th and 6th greens after he had cut the deficit to just one shot at that stage of the last round.

Standing on the 7th tee two over, Lema remarked to "Tip", "I guess we're in trouble now", to which the caddie reassured him "he's played the easy bit (The Loop), just you stay focused and it'll take care of itself". Sure enough, five consecutive threes released the pressure and he finished six under par for the last twelve holes, birdying the last with a traditional pitch and run approach shot to three feet, which delighted the crowd.

When presenting the press with half bottles of champagne (as he'd done on his five previous wins that year), Lema announced modestly that his win was 49% himself and 51% "Tip" Anderson – "He just put the club in my hand and I just hit it". Lema was understating the affair – for he had manufactured low run-up shots he would never have needed in the States, and played them like a local! It was a hugely popular win by the charismatic and elegant swinging American. The golfing world lost a great personality when, shortly after coming fourth at Birkdale in the '65 Open, Tony Lema was killed in a plane crash. He was thirty-two years old.

Arnold Palmer, feeling jaded, decided not to come over for The Open but lent Lema his caddie who steered him round the course to victory, with just one practice round.

Tony Lema receiving the trophy before champagne corks popped for the press in celebration of his win in the '64 Open.

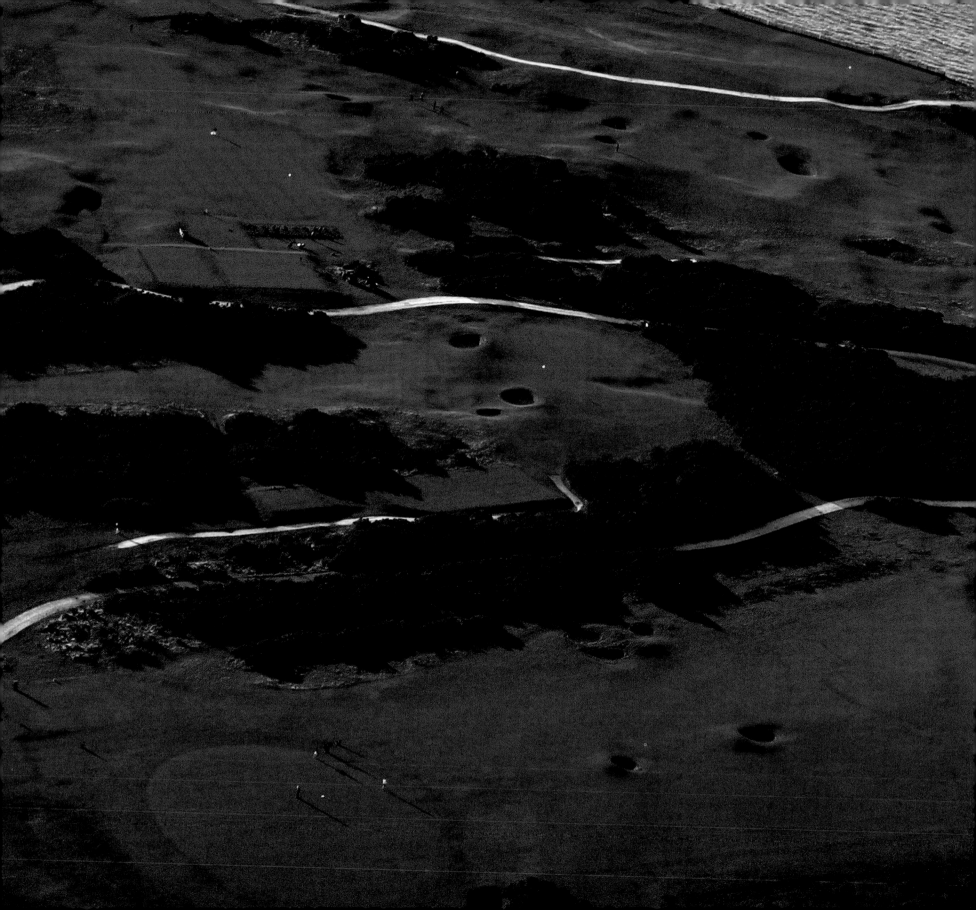

The Loop – picture of:

bottom left to right - 9th green and 10th tee, 8th and10[th] greens, 7th and 11th green.

middle left – New Course 5th green par 3.

top left – Old Course 6th and 12th greens

The battle against erosion goes on behind the 11th green where a new tee was installed for the 2005 Open, to lengthen the short par 4 12th hole. This area needed protection from the constant action of heavy waves sweeping into the estuary from the North Sea.

12th

"Heathery In"

348 yard par 4

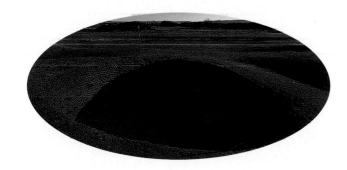

Nicklaus – back-to-back wins in 1970 and '78.

Hole # 12
"Heathery In"

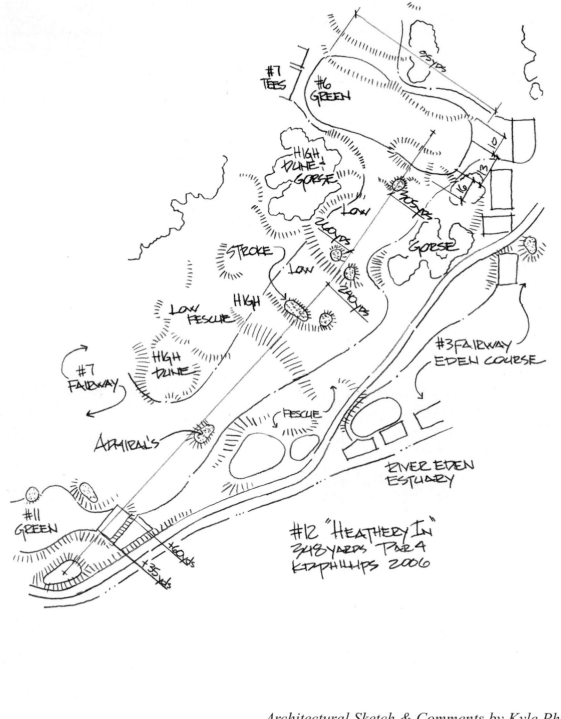

Like the 9th hole, the 12th is a short par 4 that plays away from the Eden Estuary and back towards the town of St. Andrews. And like the 9th, it appears visually to be a straightforward driving hole. But this hole is no place to relax, as the bunkers are totally hidden from view and are both deep and gathering, and if found with one's drive, a shot to par is certain to be lost.

When striding to the fairway, be careful not to tumble into "Admiral's" bunker. Looking back from the fairway toward the tee, one will begin to imagine how "Admiral's" and "Hill" bunkers come into play when the course is played in a clockwise direction.

Architectural Sketch & Comments by Kyle Phillips

This aerial view of the 12th, with "Admirals" bunker bottom right, shows all of the bunkers hidden from view from the tee.

From the 12th tee the drive looks trouble-free but there are four bunkers, hidden from view, down the length of the fairway. Only when you view the course from the direction it was originally played (in reverse of today) does this make sense (see opposite picture). In the same way, the apron greens were not there to prevent the ball from getting up onto the green, but to take it off the back of the green.

CONTENDERS IN THE 1970 OPEN

At the half-way stage Lee Trevino (left) was leading by a shot with two rounds of 68. One shot back were Tony Jacklin (right) and Jack Nicklaus. Jacklin had been the first home-based player to win the Open (since Max Faulkner in 1951) the previous year at Lytham, and was also the current US Champion.

Much was expected of him and, under enormous pressure, he rose to the challenge birdying four of the first five holes and went out in 29. Still attacking the hole on the way in, the heavens opened while he was on the 14th, flooding the course. Play was quickly suspended preventing what might have been the greatest round ever played in an Open Championship. With the momentum gone he limped in after an early start the next day bogeying three of the last five holes for a round of 67. More disappointment lay ahead for Jacklin, as Lee Trevino would rob him of the next two Opens at Birkdale and Muirfield.

Looking back through the 12th green and undulating fairway towards the tee.

SURVIVING OPEN CHAMPIONS IN THE SHADOW OF THE R & A – 1905

left to right:

J. H. Taylor 1894, '95, 1900;   Jack White 1904; Harold Hilton 1892 and '97; John Ball 1890;   James Braid 1901 and '05;   Tom Morris 1861, '62, '64 and '67; Bob Ferguson 1880, '81 and '82; Willie Auchterlonie 1893;   Jamie Anderson 1877, '78 and '79; Hugh Kirkaldy 1891; Bob Martin 1876 and '85; Willie Fernie 1883.Seated on the grass: Sandy Herd 1902; Harry Vardon 1896, '98, '99 and 1903; Willie Park Jnr 1877 and '89; Jack Simpson 1884.

THE PAST CHAMPIONS' DINNER ON THE EVE OF THE 1970 OPEN AT ST ANDREWS

left to right: Arthur Havers 1923; Gene Sarazen 1932; Dick Burton 1939; Fred Daly 1947; Roberto de Vicenzo 1967; Arnold Palmer 1961 and '62; Kel Nagle 1960; Bobby Locke 1949, '50, '52 and '57; Henry Cotton 1934, '37 and '48; Peter Thomson 1954, '55, '56, '58 and '65.   front row: Densmore Shute 1933; Bob Charles 1963; Max Faulkner 1951; Jack Nicklaus 1966; Tony Jacklin 1969; Gary Player 1959 and 1968.

J ack Nicklaus's mighty blow through green off the tee on the last hole of the play-off in the 1970 Open will always be remembered, as will Doug Sanders' putt on the 18th green that brought it about! He just needed a four to win, but who could forget the tension as he deliberated – stopped – and started again, over a three-foot putt to save par. It wandered off right of the hole and away from the R & A, the presentation table and the Claret Jug!

In blustery conditions only twenty-five players broke 70 in the first round, but only two managed that in the stiff breeze of the third round. After Nicklaus chipped up short from the rough at the back of that final green of the eighteen hole play-off on the Sunday, Sanders was still in with a chance. Nicklaus holed a ten footer to close out the luckless Sanders, who was nearly "brained" by the descent of his adversary's putter which had just about reached orbit, thrown up in the air, in a release of tension, when the putt dropped in. Sanders then proceeded to tap in a similar putt to the one he'd missed the day before, but was already beaten.

When asked thirty-five years later if he still thought about "that missed putt", he replied casually that he hadn't thought of it once …. during his lunch that day!

Jack Nicklaus in 1978   1970 driving the 18th green

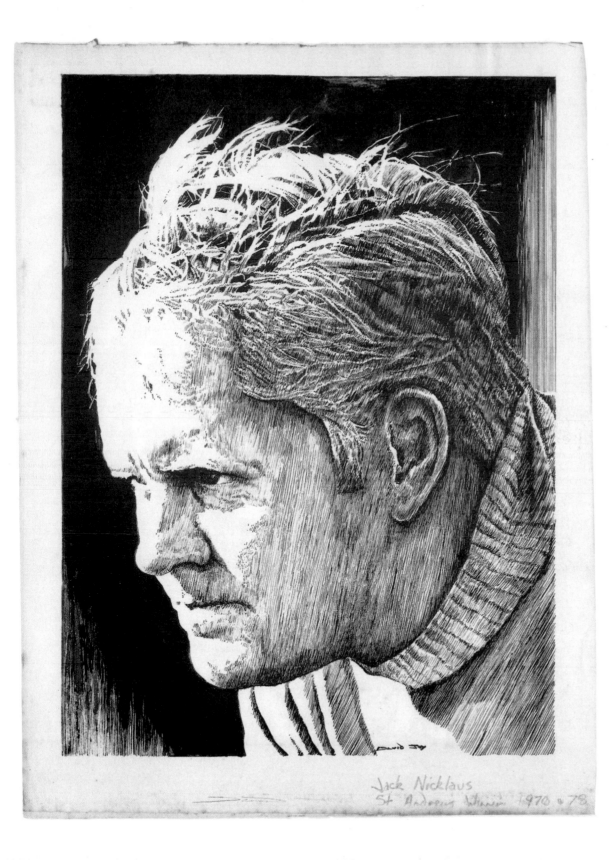

Jack Nicklaus
St Andrews Winner 1970 & 78

I ntense concentration during the 1970 Open.

Although the high standard of Nicklaus's game and his persona did not change from his win at St Andrews in 1970 – to successfully defending his title again there in '78 – his looks did.

Gone was the intimidating presence of the man – replaced by a more casual and coiffured Jack Nicklaus. He acknowledged yet another "Major" win on the steps between the last hole and the R & A, to an ecstatic crowd. From one St Andrews win to the other he had finished 5th, 2nd, 4th, 3rd, 3rd, 2nd and 2nd again, in an epic battle named "The Duel in the Sun" against Tom Watson at Turnberry.

Gary Player, as a young South African, played his first Open at St Andrews in 1955. He went on to win three in three decades - 1959 at Muirfield, '68 at Carnoustie and '74 at Lytham and was part of "The Big Three" along with Nicklaus and Palmer in many televised matches in the 60s.

As well as his consistently high finishes in the Opens between his two wins at St Andrews, Jack Nicklaus picked up two Masters and three PGA titles, as well as seventy-six other tournament wins on the American circuit!

The 1978 Open was truly international when at the half-way stage Japan made an impact for the first time in a Major; Aoki was joint leader on five under with Azoki and Nakajima just two shots behind. Ballesteros was up there for Spain as was Australian Shearer. Also in the mix were Americans: Crenshaw, Weiskopf and Kite; followed by Palmer and Moody. In with a chance representing Britain were Oosterhuis and Faldo - Nicklaus was four off the pace. At one point in the third round five tied for the lead.

After much too-ing and fro-ing "Big Jack" emerged a worthy winner yet again with two imperious final rounds of 68, drawing on his vast experience, absorbing the pressure and rising to the big occasion.

Nicklaus holds the Claret Jug aloft after winning again at St Andrews in 1978.

13th

"Hole O' Cross In"

465 yard par 4

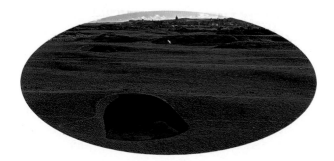

"Olé!" – Seve Ballesteros in 1984.

Hole #13
"Hole O'Cross In"

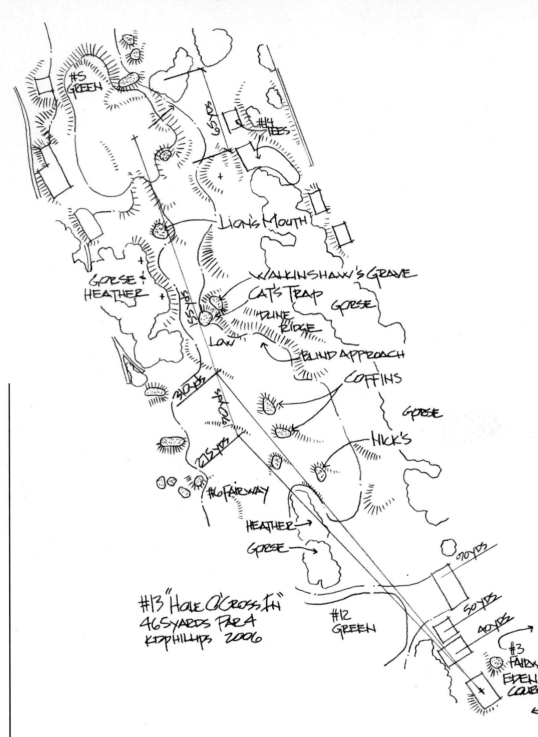

#5 GREEN

65YDS

#4 TEES

LION'S MOUTH

GORSE & HEATHER

WALKINSHAW'S GRAVE

CATS TRAP

157YDS

DUNE RIDGE

GORSE

LOW

BLIND APPROACH

COFFINS

310YDS

GORSE

270YDS

NICK'S

235YDS

#6 FAIRWAY

HEATHER →

GORSE →

#13 "Hole O'Cross In"
465 YARDS PAR 4
KD PHILLIPS 2006

#12 GREEN

70YDS

50YDS

40YDS

#3 FAIRWAY EDEN COURSE

Architectural Sketch & Comments by Kyle Phillips

L ocals say that the true challenge of the Old Course begins on the 13th tee. This risk and reward option tee shot offers the immediate hazard of "Nick's" bunker and "The Coffins", positioned between the 13th and 6th fairway. Take on and clear the bunkers and the reward is a relatively simple approach shot to this large green. Any player aiming right of the bunkers must consider the angle of the long natural dune that indents into the fairway. This high landform forces long drives to the left and towards the bunkers, while hiding the view of the green from the approach shot. Add to all of this the variable wind, and this stands out as one of the great natural terrain routings in the game of golf.

Opposite: The 13th fairway, bordered to the right by gorse bushes, has the fearsome "Nick's" and "Coffins" bunkers directly in line with the preferred line towards the green.

The 13th is one of the most challenging and perhaps underrated holes on the Old Course. The early morning light highlights and shadows areas of rough, bunkers, fairway, green and the distant skyline of the town, to dramatic effect.

THE 1984 OPEN

Above: Lifting the trophy for the fifth time in 1983 at Birkdale. As in 1978 at St Andrews, Watson was again defending the Championship.

Right: Tom Watson, following through on a long iron shot.

In the build-up to The Open at St Andrews, all the talk was about whether Watson could equal Vardon's long-standing record of six wins. It was a great achievement, in modern-day terms, for Watson to be in a position to even threaten that record. Given the high quality of the field during his era it was surprising that only Ballesteros in 1978 and Bill Rogers in 1981 had been able to break his outstanding run of play.

After an immaculate score of 66 in the third round, Watson found himself in the familiar position of playing "last couple" on the final day! At 1.46 pm he drove off with Ian Baker-Finch (both on 11 under) in search of immortality. Teeing up at the 12th it looked achievable, with only Ballesteros threatening, after a bad start from Baker-Finch and the only other real contender, Bernhard Langer, struggling to

find form with his putter. Watson hit an uncharacteristic drive at that hole and found a whin bush which forced a penalty drop.

Now it was really getting down to the wire. The Spaniard, playing one hole in front, birdied the par 5 14th – Watson did likewise at the difficult 13th. Ballesteros, although still young, was tough and relished what was to develop into a match play situation in the short battle that lay ahead. As a typical seaside breeze got up he donned his "lucky navy blue sweater" the one worn when playing at Lytham and at The Masters the year before.

They both parred 15 and 16 and were level with each other. The 17th hole, which had terrified players throughout its history, would yet again decide the outcome of a close encounter. Seve drove left, flirting dangerously with the rough, but luckily found a good lie. Pumped up, with adrenalin flowing, he hit a majestic six iron 200 yards into the heart of the green, and with two putts put the pressure back on.

Watson, in turn, had to wait for an agonising minute to find out whether his ball was out of bounds having taken a tight line over The Old Course Hotel off the 17th tee. His ball was in play and, in fact, in a perfect spot, on the right-hand side of the fairway, for attacking the flag. He looked calm as he lined up for yet another "most important shot of his life". As he was about to hit the ball, a roar went up, signalling that Seve was close to the pin on his final shot to the last green. Watson settled again but had over-clubbed with a two iron and pushed the shot badly to the worst position he could have imagined – in a bad lie over the road, behind the green and just two feet from the wall.

He did well to scuttle the ball up towards the flag but had left a swinging ten yard putt that would not drop. His heart must have sank as he witnessed, in the distance, Ballesteros's successful birdie putt and heard the delight of the crowd as the Spaniard saluted them with that unforgettable "Olé".

Top Right: A young Seve Ballesteros looks pensive as he waits to play after two rounds of 69 and 70 in the 1978 Open at St Andrews – he was tying with Crenshaw and Aoki for the lead at that time.

Right: Seve's cavalier style of play throughout his career was backed by his uncanny knack of getting "up and down" from the most unlikely places.

"Olé"

14th

"Long"

618 yard par 5

Faldo grinds it out to win in 1990.

Hole #14 – "Long"

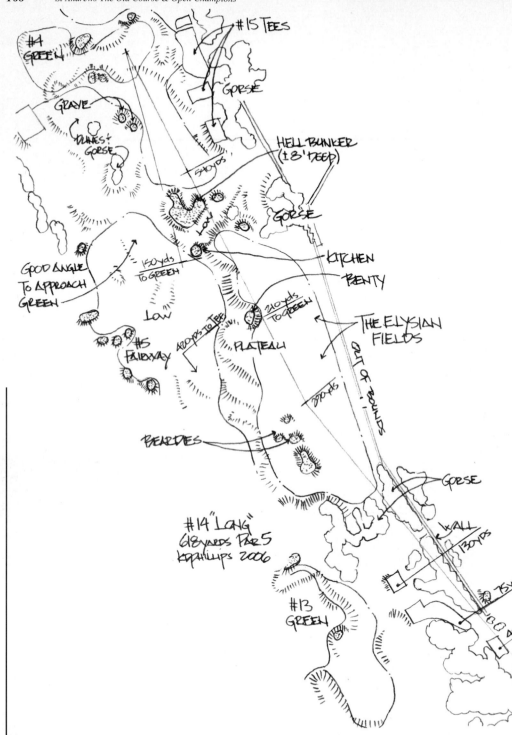

The labels on the sketch read:

#4 GREEN

#15 TEES

GORSE

GRAVE

DUNES + GORSE

HELL BUNKER (±8' DEEP)

GORSE

150yds TO GREEN

GOOD ANGLE TO APPROACH GREEN

KITCHEN PLENTY

LOW

LOW

THE ELYSIAN FIELDS

420YDS TO TEE

210 yds TO GREEN

#5 FAIRWAY

PLATEAU

OUT OF BOUNDS

390 yds

BEARDIES

GORSE

WALL 130 YDS

75YDS

#14 "LONG" 618 YARDS PAR 5 KP PHILLIPS 2006

130 YDS

40YDS

#13 GREEN

The drive is dominated by the wall and out-of-bounds running down the right and the "Beardies" bunkers down the left. With a favourable breeze, only the longest drives into the Elysian Fields have the opportunity to play directly for the green. The second shots must recognize the presence of the cavernous "Hell" bunker and when the wind is unfavourable many second shots will be seen played left across the large saw-tooth ledge and down into the 5th fairway. Even when the winds are not an issue, locals frequently play their second shot to the areas left of "Hell" bunker (the 5th fairway), as from this position the ridges of the green are favourable for the approach shot.

Opposite: The wide, flat, expanse of the Elysian Fields, on the 14th fairway, is bordered on the right by the out-of-bounds wall – with the "Beardies" bunkers bottom left.

Architectural Sketch & Comments by Kyle Phillips

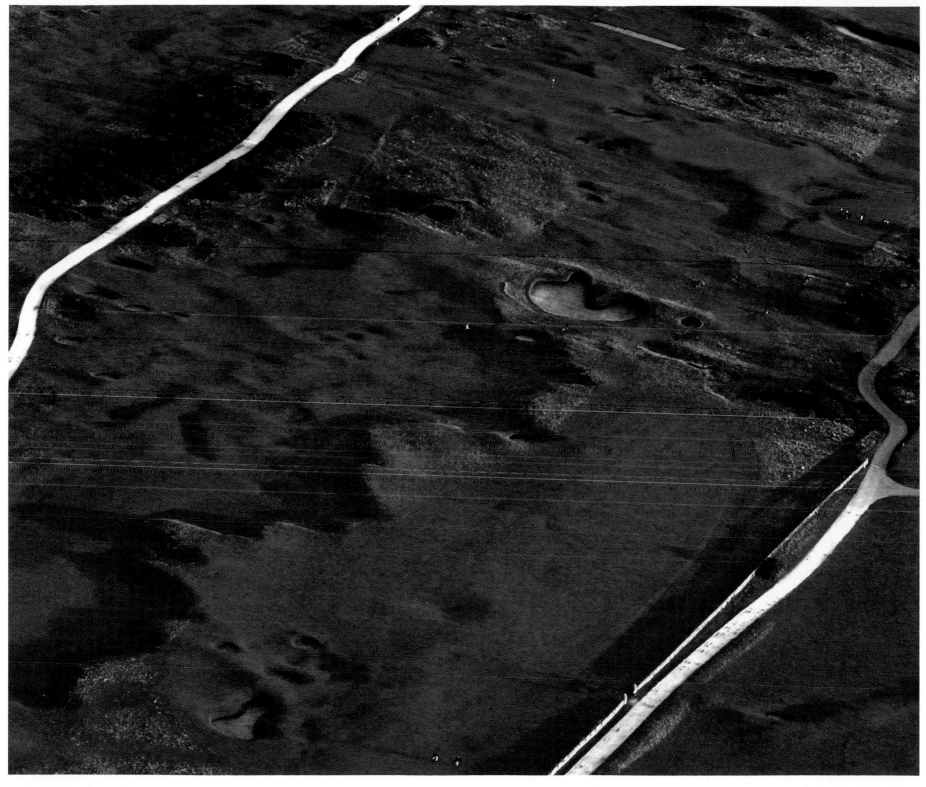

Two photographs to show the seasonal comparison from the 14th tee to the Elysian Fields and town, where sunlight shadows the buildings from 3 pm on a winter afternoon, but they remain bathed in a golden light until 9 pm on a summer's evening. This tee shot must avoid the "out-of-bounds" wall to the right and "The Beardies" three bunkers, in close proximity to each other, but out of sight to the left.

Below: "Hell" bunker 2005

Opposite: "Hell" bunker 1886

Double Page: "Hell" bunker today

HELL BUNKER—OLD COURSE.

[From a photo by J. Patrick & Son, Edinburgh.]

Sunlight and shadows on the 14th green show how well it is protected by steep slopes to the front of the green.

THE 1990 OPEN

It was an outstanding Open for Nick Faldo, who played immaculate golf over all four days. His only blemish was to catch the greenside bunker by the 4th green in the final round. It was outstanding for various reasons, as records tumbled during the week. A record-equalling aggregate for the first two rounds by Faldo and Greg Norman of 132 (Henry Cotton had done it in 1934); a record lowest score of 63 by Englishman Paul Broadhurst; record crowds of over 200,000; record prize money which had nearly doubled from 1984 (£825,000); Faldo shooting less than 200 in three rounds and St Andrews equalling Prestwick's old record of hosting 24 Championships.

Arnold Palmer came in on level par at the half-way stage and although he received a hero's welcome, it was slightly subdued for spectators were saving themselves for the final day to show their real appreciation of Palmer's last Open at St Andrews. It was not to be as yet another record was broken in the lowest cut at one under. Luckily he returned in '95 and bid a proper farewell. Watson and Ballesteros paired together for the first two rounds were also major casualties, but Nicklaus just squeezed through and made the final day for the 28th time.

On the last day Baker-Finch was yet again in the final pairing, at an Open, after a third round 64. He would win the next year, but from then on struggled to find his game. Payne Stewart got to within three shots but drove into the dreaded "Coffin" Bunker at the 13th and fell away. Only Mark McNulty surged through the field with seven birdies and no dropped shots in a tricky easterly wind.

Not since the great Harry Vardon's early pioneering days across to The States, at the turn of the century, had a British player made such an impact on both sides of the water as Nick Faldo. He was justifiably ranked No 1 in the world after his win at St Andrews.

15th

"Cartgate In"

456 yard par 4

John Daly tames the wind in 1995.

Hole #15 – "Cartgate In"

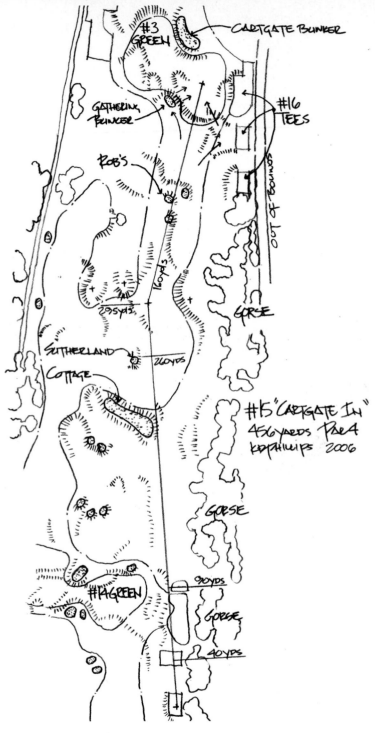

CARTGATE BUNKER

#3 GREEN

GATHERING BUNKER

#16 TEES

OUT OF BOUNDS

ROB'S

GORSE

150yds

295yds

SUTHERLAND COTTAGE

260yds

#15 "CARTGATE IN"
456 yards Par 4
KP Phillips 2006

GORSE

#14 GREEN

90yds

GORSE

40yds

The ideal line is down the right centre of the fairway. A line left off the tee over the "Cottage" bunker into the wide part of the fairway must avoid the "Sutherland" bunker that looms behind. The fairway turns slightly right and narrows between dune and gorse approximately 160 yards from the green. Second shots can make use of the open entry green for run up approaches, but must avoid the gathering front left greenside bunker.

Architectural Sketch & Comments by Kyle Phillips

The 15th is defined by "Cottage" bunker (bottom left) and the semi-circular "Cartgate" bunker at the back of the 15th and 3rd green. Beyond, following the footpath (old railway line), is the 16th.

The approach to the 15th green.

O n the 25th Anniversary of Opens played at St Andrews in 1995, John Daly mastered a persistently nagging wind that blew all week. It was his deft touch around the green rather than his immense power that won him the Championship.

Scoring was unpredictable. Old favourite Tom Watson had an impressive first round of 67 when he scored 31 on the back nine – Daly, Crenshaw and McNulty also scored posted 67s that day. Faldo made a move on the second day when he too scored a 67. In round three Campbell charged through the field to nine under. Elkington was up there with his second 69 of the three rounds, but in the last round it was like shuffling a pack of cards to decide the outcome – until late on, when Italian Costontina Rocca emerged as Daly's biggest threat. It was to be yet another great climax to The Open Championship. Big John removed at least two feet of sand getting out of the "Road Hole" Bunker but dropped a shot – Rocca playing behind him was also in trouble at the 17th. Playing off the road, behind the green, he jumped the ball up a grassy slope to within four feet and holed the putt for par. Suddenly he found himself needing a three up the last to tie. Under pressure he fluffed a chip – almost apologetically, into the Valley of Sin and as Daly was thinking about his acceptance speech, holed the most unlikely of putts ever seen. As Rocca sank to his knees in disbelief the roar from the crowd must have been heard in Carnoustie. A four-hole play-off followed immediately with neither man having much time to compose himself. After Daly holed a thirty footer at the 2nd and Rocca three stabbed in the "Road Hole" Bunker at the next, the title was won, and John Daly in time-honoured fashion acknowledged the crowd on his victory march down the last.

Above: John Daly winding up on the 8th tee. Right: "The St Andrews Swing"! Compare the similarities between Hugh Kirkaldy's when winning in 1891 and that of Daly today.

G reg Norman (right) and Nick Faldo (above) bring back memories of their epic duel on the Saturday afternoon of the 1990 Open Championship.

Having played in a relentlessly strong wind in the Scottish Open at Carnoustie the week before, US Amateur Champion Tiger Woods found himself yet again exposed to the elements at St Andrews. He finished seven over par, and back in the Clubhouse two hours before the eventual winner.

Striding down the 18th fairway, Arnold Palmer had said his last farewell from the Swilken Bridge, thirty-five years after leaving his mark in The Centenary Open.

Driving off the last tee, American Payne Stewart, in all his sartorial elegance, was well up with the pace again after two rounds. His stylish play and colourful attire were sadly missed when, like Tony Lema before him, he was tragically killed in a plane crash at the height of his career.

16th

"Corner of the Dyke"

424 yard par 4

Enter the Tiger! The 2000 Millennium Open.

Hole #16
"Corner of the Dyke"

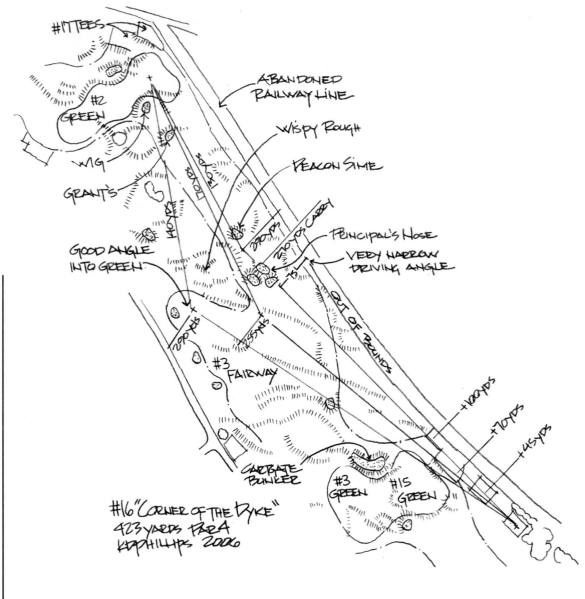

#17 TEES

#2 GREEN

MG

GRANT'S

GOOD ANGLE INTO GREEN

ABANDONED RAILWAY LINE

WISPY ROUGH

DEACON SIME

PRINCIPAL'S NOSE

VERY NARROW DRIVING ANGLE

OUT OF BOUNDS

#3 FAIRWAY

CARTGATE BUNKER

#3 GREEN

#15 GREEN

+100 YDS

+70 YDS

+45 YDS

#16 "CORNER OF THE DYKE"
423 YARDS PAR 4
KYLE PHILLIPS 2006

The tee shot plays on slight left to right diagonal making for a very difficult driving hole. The angle of the slope that cuts across the green favours an approach from the left side of the fairway. A long drive must either carry over the "Principal's Nose" bunker and run left of "Deacon Sime" bunker or carry near the out-of-bounds on the right in order to miss "Deacon Sime" on the left. Alternatively, drives can be played long and left into the 3rd fairway, then played blind over heather, gorse and bunkers to the green that is ridged to the front at an angle favourable to a left approach.

Architectural Sketch & Comments by Kyle Phillips

The view from the 16th tee to green, out-of-bounds right and "Principal's Nose" bunker centre.

The Principal's Nose

The raised 16th green with out-of-bounds to the right and pot bunkers to the left.

James Braid playing off the railway line beside the 16th on his way to winning in 1905.

The Millennium Open was the 129th in the Championship's history. That week Tiger Woods left his mark on the history of the game – when his 19 under par total at St Andrews was a fitting climax to winning all The Majors, back to back. Having won the US Open at Pebble Beach before his decisive victory in The British Open, he then proceeded to take the US PGA title yet again that year. As the golfing fraternity wondered who could possibly knock Tom Morris

Jnr, aged twenty four, off his pedestal – it was happening again one hundred and twenty-five years later!! Woods was relentlessly stepping up the ladder and had already joined Nicklaus, Hogan, Player and Sarazen as the only winners of all four Major trophies.

Tiger Woods left a strong field in his wake when mastering The Old. Despite the old saying "the course starts at the 13th", it was a triumphant march up the home holes in the last round by Woods to win by eight shots from his nearest rivals, Ernie Els and Thomas Bjorn. David Duval looked like his only real challenger, at one time reducing the lead to three shots, birdying four of the first seven holes in the final round. Tiger stepped up a gear and birdied the 10th and 12th as Duval, playing with him bogeyed them both; to add insult to injury he was savaged by the "Road Hole" bunker on the 17th when he took four to get out of it. Tiger's course management throughout the week was impeccable, and at no time did he even flirt with any of the one hundred and twenty-six deep-faced bunkers.

They had all played in ideal conditions – bright sunshine and no wind. Apart from the exceptional scoring of Woods, it was reassuring that the Old Course had withstood the challenge of the world's best players to take her down a peg or two.

Looking back through the 16th green to the 15th and 3rd, 14th and 4th, and 13th and 5th double greens, and beyond to the snow-capped Sidlaw hills, in the next county, dusted with snow.

A panoramic view of St Andrews and the Old Course. The 16th green sits beside the left-hand side of the Old Course Hotel, and the 17th green to the right.

PARADE OF CHAMPIONS

On the eve of The Millennium Open, before the traditional Past Champions Dinner hosted by the R & A, all the previous winners assembled and played an exhibition match of two holes out and two holes in. A vast crowd packed the arena and applauded their every move. Apart from the notable absence of Arnold Palmer, it was a unique and memorable occasion. Who said nostalgia isn't what it used to be?!

Acknowledging the crowds as they march down the first are (from left to right)

Top: Lee Trevino – 1971 and '72, Tony Jacklin 1969, Gary Player 1959, '68 and '74 and Seve Ballesteros 1979, '84 and '88.

Middle: Veteran Sam Snead, who won at St Andrews in 1946, was paired with Nick Faldo, 1987, '90 and '92.

Bottom: Tom Watson, followed by Jack Nicklaus, receives a commemorative silver salver for the event from the outgoing Secretary to the R & A, Sir Michael Bonallack.

17th

"Road"

455 yard par 4

Tiger Woods becomes the fifth double-winner at St Andrews in 2005.

Hole #17 – "Road"

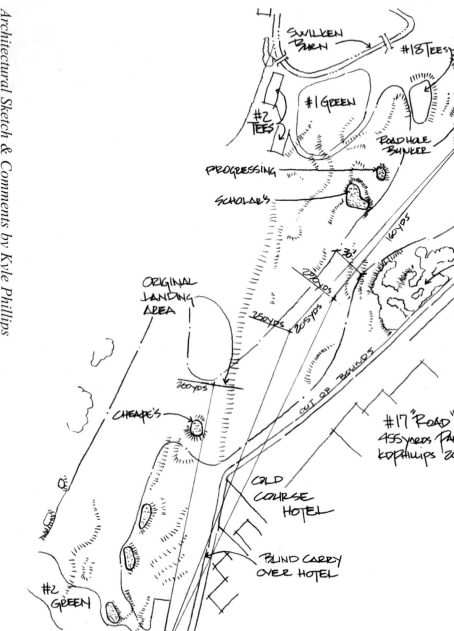

This 455 yard dog-leg right par 4 is arguably the most famous hole in golf and one that challenges the abilities of all golfers. Originally it was a three shot hole with a brave drive playing just over the corner of the wall. It was played as a par 5 until the mid 1960s when the ability to bite off more and more of the corner shortened the hole to a long iron approach. As technology advances and drives fly longer, the fairway continues to be narrowed. During The Open Championship, portions of the fairway are reduced in width to the point of being not much wider than a foot path.

On arrival at the tee, one is faced with a completely blind tee shot over what was once old railway sheds and is now The Old Course Hotel. The drive is intimidating not only because of the out-of-bounds on the right, but because anything to the left will run through the fairway into long grass and heather.

The approach shot is mind boggling; a narrow long green at right angles to the fairway; one deep pot bunker to the front (with gathering contours); a road directly behind the green and an out-of-bounds wall just beyond. Even with the perfect drive to the fairway, the approach shot, with a medium to long iron, seems akin to threading a golf ball through the eye of a needle.

An elevated view of the 17th tee to green, further dramatised by passing storm-clouds and Autumnal colours.

Any tee shot overshooting the fairway left, will find it difficult to clear "Scholars" bunker and get onto the green safely.

This is a familiar view which creates a problem for so many players who find themselves here for two; there really is no simple "up and down" to save par. Any attempt to putt towards the general direction of the flag will be gathered by the steep contouring of "The Devils Swale", into the "Road" bunker, while an attempted "lob" flick, over the bunker, requires a level of accuracy beyond the ability of most mere mortals! This is three putt territory, accept a five and enjoy the view.

This detailed sketch of the 17th may help to unravel some of the mystery that surrounds one of the toughest par 4's in golf.

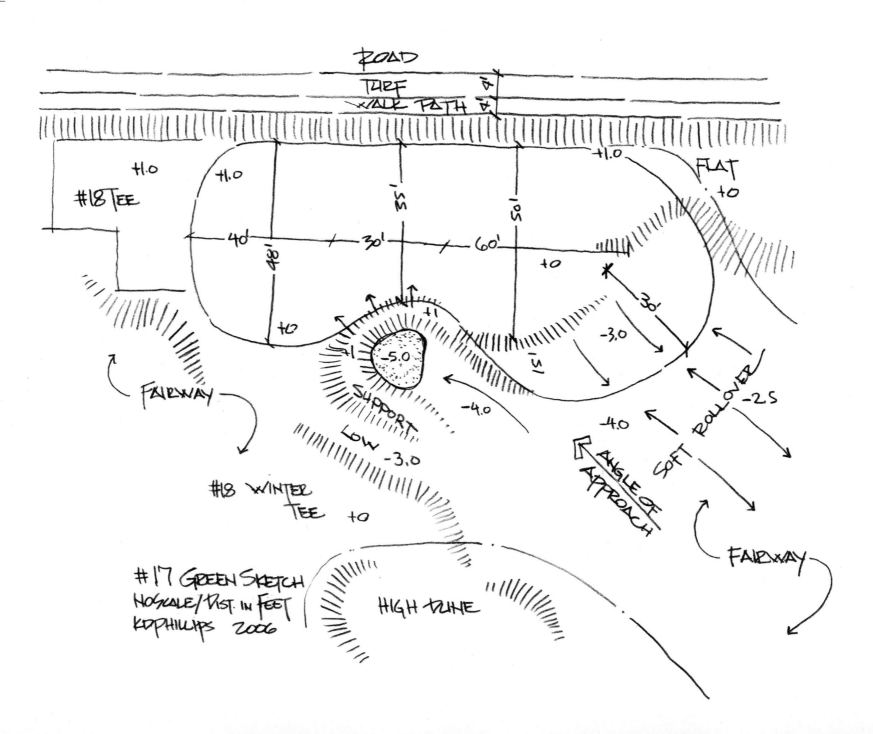

It was still "tight at the turn" on the last round of the 2005 Championship, with Colin Montgomerie hanging on to the belief that he could still win his first elusive major. Despite the encouragement of a huge home-based crowd it wasn't to be, as Tiger stepped up a gear. By the 15th tee he was five shots ahead in a tricky wind that had many struggling. Olazabel had been in contention and battled hard, finishing joint third with Fred Couples who, with a 68, had jumped up the leader board. Tiger finished on fourteen under par – yet again a worthy winner. With a philosophical shrug of the shoulders Montgomerie picked up the runner-up cheque for £430,000 and the silver salver, ready to fight again another day.

Ernie Els, joint runner-up to Tiger Woods in 2005, won at Muirfield three years before.

The "Road Hole" bunker claims another victim, although in this case New Zealander Michael Campbell gets up and down for his par.

Tiger Woods becomes the fifth double winner at St Andrews in 2005.

After receiving the Claret Jug for the second time in 2005, along with a cheque for £750,000, Tiger Woods said in his acceptance speech, "Today was an incredible battle. To somehow play a little better was amazing. A dream come true. It is truly an honour to play at the Home of Golf." *Inset:* Peter Thomson – five times Open Champion – was introduced to the crowd at the presentation, in recognition of the 50th anniversary of his win at St Andrews.

18th

"Tom Morris"

354 yard par 4

The Home Hole

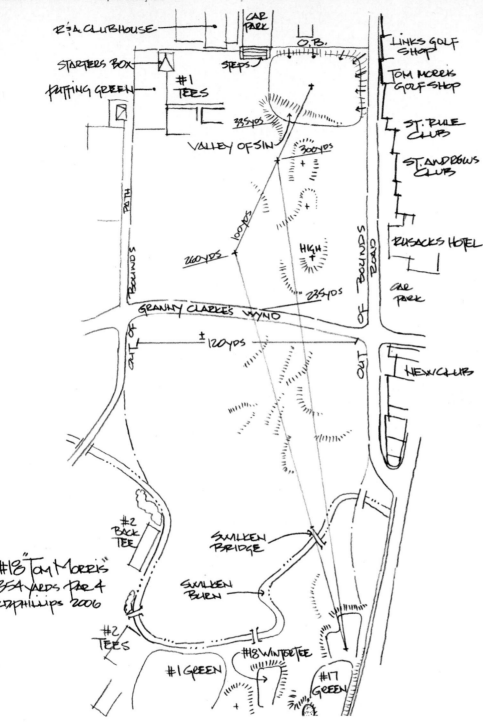

Hole #18
"Tom Morris"

The final hole is simply the grand stage of golf. The drive plays from just off the 17th green, across the Swilken Burn and Granny Clark's Wynd, into a backdrop of the Clubhouse of the Royal & Ancient Golf Club. With the prodigious distances the professionals are driving the ball today, they all seem to favour playing long and left, hoping to play their short second shot from the Valley of Sin. Long John Daly nearly lost the Open by driving the ball out of bounds beyond the green. But fortunately for him, the ball rebounded safely back down the steps leading to the R & A Clubhouse, leaving him a short pitch to the green.

As one crosses the Swilken Bridge for the obligatory photo with the Royal & Ancient Clubhouse behind, old buildings consisting of residences, hotels and shops running down the right, always provide a historical gallery for one's imaginary winning putt at the next Open Championship.

Architectural Sketch & Comments by Kyle Phillips

The 18th fairway, burnt to a links brown. The traditional line from the tee is to aim on the R & A clock.

The late-evening sun bathes the 18th green and R & A Clubhouse, as shadows lengthen into the Valley of Sin – a popular resting place for so many!

The dramatic undulations of the 18th fairway shadowed by the late-evening sun are completely lost to the golfer

who is focused only on the birdie putt.

THE PAST AND PRESENT

"The Home Hole" was re-named "Tom Morris" after his retiral in 1902. What would Young and Old Tom make of this travelling circus that comes to town now, compared with that first Open they played in on the Old Course in 1873? The 26 entrants simply put their names forward (no entry fee) and checked the ballot the next day to see when they would play! Now there are international qualifying rounds across five continents and qualifying rounds to play to pre-qualify for the regional qualifying to qualify for the qualifying rounds on the week of the Open!!!

It's a far cry from the first national report of the Open at St Andrews, in 1885, when the chief reporter of the Daily Mail complained about the time of year it was held (October) and his shock that amateurs were beaten by professionals! I quote 'The great golfers' meeting at St Andrews is just over. Why has the season of the equinoctial gales been chosen for this contest by a club that is Royal and Ancient? Furious and tyrannical weather has not even the advantage of keeping women away from the scene. Out they come in mackintoshes and deer-stalking caps in their legions.

How can we attribute such a terrible defeat of gentlemen by players in this late Championship? The differentia, on good judicial authority, is stated thus –"The gentlemen player wears gloves. The professional does not wear gloves – and spits on his hands" '. *Above:* Tom Morris Senior and Junior, 1870.

Some time after the Millennium Open Jack Nicklaus asked the Championship Secretary when it would be back in St Andrews; he was told 2006. Nicklaus remarked that was a pity as he would be sixty-six (past Champions up to sixty-five years old were exempt from qualifying). Lo and behold, shortly after, it was announced that the Open would return one year earlier!

It was a fitting farewell as Nicklaus was clapped all the way round the course on the Friday afternoon. The applause became rapturous by the 17th and built up to a crescendo. As emotions ran high he holed one last birdie putt on the last green and bowed out with dignity.

At a packed press conference after his final farewell, Jack Nicklaus talked - as had Bobby Jones many years before him – about his love of the Old Course, and how it was the most appropriate place to sign off from competitive golf.

From 1959, when he won the US Amateur, to winning the Masters for the sixth and final time in 1986 – he amassed over 70 tournament victories in the States; 18 worldwide and 20 Majors, in a long and illustrious career.

There is an almost carnival atmosphere in the town when St Andrews hosts an Open.   When spectators spill out onto the street from the pubs around Golf Place at the end of a day's play, there is great camaraderie and humour and no trouble whatsoever. The galleries that flock in their thousands to see the Open are the most knowledgeable in the world of golf.

Everybody has their own favourites, as can be seen here with Nicklaus' and Montgomerie's "groupies" (dressed for the occasion). But there's never any animosity as a true champion is appreciated by all.

SPECTATORS

Five hundred locals frequently turned up to watch the members of the St Andrews Society of Golfers (the R & A) be piped down from the cobbled end of Market Street to the course for their Spring and Autumn Meetings of the late eighteenth century.

Large crowds gathered for Challenge and Foursomes matches, when Morris and Robertson, representing St Andrews, took on all comers in the 1850s. Train loads of supporters would travel the short distance from Edinburgh to Musselburgh to cheer on the Park brothers – or further down the line to North Berwick, where the Dunn brothers were formidable opponents. Such was the build-up and hype to those challenge matches that fierce rivalry and heavy on-course betting led to unruly behaviour and, at times, was physically threatening to the players! During one match at Musselburgh, Tom Morris sought refuge in Mrs Foreman's pub during the round and refused to come out until Willie Park's followers calmed down.

At the first Open here in St Andrews galleries were respectful, but by the mid 1880s they were getting out of hand. The problem was that without stewardship, spectators could, and

did, roam freely about the course, blocking greens and obstructing players. By the turn of the century it was positively dangerous to win The Open, as James Braid would testify. He was swamped by a surging euphoric crowd after winning the fiftieth anniversary Open in 1910 and must have feared for his life. Harry Vardon, the record six-times winner of The Open, had to shield his ball from stampeding feet down the 13th fairway as they rushed past to see "The Boy Wonder", Bobby Jones, emerge from "the loop" in the 1921 championship. To prevent him being crushed, Jones was carried aloft from the last green, holding his putter "Calamity Jane" above his head after his emphatic win in 1927. Just two years earlier, Prestwick had hosted its last Open, despite having been its original home. The venue could no longer cope with the crowds that descended on it. Five times Open winner, J. H. Taylor described how MacDonald Smith had returned from America to his native Scotland, only to lose a six shot lead going into the final round. Taylor said, "It was unfortunate for Mac that 15,000 spectators

stopped him winning. He was timed to start just when the Glasgow trains were disgorging their human cargo onto the inadequate platform. The result was that thousands jumped the intervening wall and he was bustled and jostled and hemmed in by the whooping multitude all the way round. He was given little room to swing and not once was he allowed the opportunity of seeing the results of his longer shots."

"Jumping the burn" was always the best way of ensuring a good view from the traditional rush up the last hole of the Old Course at St Andrews as the Championship reached its climax. Now over 200,000 spectators are expected over seven days with at least 20,000 stand seats provided. The town and surrounding area is inundated with requests for accommodation. For example, renting houses for The Open is handled officially by a local solicitor's firm, who start taking bookings two years before the event and end up dealing with about 1,000 properties. I am not suggesting that there is a mass exodus of people giving up their homes for the Championship, but there does seem to be an unusually large number of postcards arriving at the local post office near the end of that week from Spain or more exotic parts!

With Hoylake having made a welcome return to The Open circuit after nearly forty years, nine venues are now used. This will hopefully ensure that each championship course is host once, with St Andrews twice in a decade.

1927 Open stampede - does she make it across the Swilken? He's got no chance!

The drama of the final moments of an Open Championship at St Andrews.

THE ST ANDREWS OPEN CHAMPIONSHIPS

1st	1873	1. TOM KIDD	ST ANDREWS	91, 88	179
		2. JAMIE ANDERSON	ST ANDREWS	91, 89	180
		3. TOM MORRIS JNR	ST ANDREWS		183

2nd	1876	1. BOB MARTIN	ST ANDREWS	86, 90	176
		2. DAVE STRATH	NORTH BERWICK	86, 90	176
		(Strath conceded a walkover)			
		3. WILLIE PARK SNR	MUSSELBURGH	94, 89	183

3rd	1879	1. JAMIE ANDERSON	ST ANDREWS	84, 85	169
		2. ANDREW KIRKALDY)	ST ANDREWS	86, 86	172
		JAMIE ALLAN)	WESTWARD HO!	88, 84	
		(Kirkaldy won the eighteen-hole play-off for 2nd)			

4th	1882	1. BOB FERGUSON	MUSSELBURGH	83, 88	171
		2. WILLIE FERNIE	DUMFRIES	88, 86	174
		3. JAMIE ANDERSON	ST ANDREWS	87, 88	175

5th	1885	1. BOB MARTIN	ST ANDREWS	84, 87	171
		2. ARCHIE SIMPSON	CARNOUSTIE	83, 89	172
		3. DAVID AYTON	ST ANDREWS	89, 85	174

6th	1888	1. JACK BURNS	WARWICK	86, 85	171
		2. DAVID ANDERSON)	ST ANDREWS	86, 86	172
		BEN SAYERS)	NORTH BERWICK	85, 87	

7th	1891	1. HUGH KIRKALDY	ST ANDREWS	83, 83	166
		2. ANDREW KIRKALDY)	ST ANDREWS	84, 84	168
		WILLIE FERNIE)	TROON	84, 84	

8th	1895	1. J. H. TAYLOR	WINCHESTER	86, 78, 80, 78	322
		2. SANDY HERD	HUDDERSFIELD	82, 77, 82, 85	326
		3. ANDREW KIRKALDY	ST ANDREWS	81, 83, 84, 84	332
9th	1900	1. J. H. TAYLOR	RICHMOND	79, 77, 78, 75	309
		2. HARRY VARDON	GANTON	79, 81, 80, 77	317
		3. JAMES BRAID	ROMFORD	82, 81, 80, 79	322
10th	1905	1. JAMES BRAID	WALTON HEATH	81, 78, 78, 81	318
		2. ROWLAND JONES)	WIMBLEDON PARK	81, 77, 87, 78	323
		J. H. TAYLOR)	MID SURREY	80, 85, 78, 80	
11th	1910	1. JAMES BRAID	WALTON HEATH	76, 73, 74, 76	299
		2. SANDY HERD	HUDDERSFIELD	78, 74, 75, 76	303
		3. GEORGE DUNCAN	HANGER HILL	73, 77, 71, 83	304
12th	1921	1. JOCK HUTCHISON	GLENVIEW - USA	72, 75, 79, 70	296
		MR R. H. WETHRED	R & A	78, 75, 72, 71	
			Play off HUTCHISON	74, 76	150
			WETHERED	77, 82	159
13th	1927	1. MR R. T. JONES	ATLANTA - USA	68, 72, 73, 72	285
		2. AUBREY BOOMER)	ST CLOUD - FRANCE	76, 70, 73, 72	291
		FRED ROBSON)	COODEN BEACH	76, 72, 69, 74	
14th	1933	1. DENSMORE SHUTE	USA	73, 73, 73, 73	292
		CRAIG WOOD	USA	77, 72, 68, 75	
			Play off SHUTE	75, 74	
			WOOD	78, 76	
15th	1939	1. DICK BURTON	SALE	70, 72, 71, 71	290
		2. JOHNNY BULLA	CHICAGO - USA	77, 71, 71, 73	292
		3. JOHNNY FALCON	HUDDERSFIELD	71, 73, 71, 79	294

16th	1946	1. SAM SNEAD	USA	71, 70, 74, 75	290
		2. BOBBY LOCKE)	S. AFRICA	69, 74, 75, 76	294
		JOHNNY BULLA)	USA	71, 72, 72, 79	

17th	1955	1. PETER THOMSON	AUSTRALIA	71, 68, 70, 72	281
		2. JOHNNY FALCON	HUDDERSFIELD	73, 67, 73, 70	283
		3. FRANK JONGE	EDGBASTON	70, 71, 69, 74	284

18th	1957	1. BOBBY LOCKE	S. AFRICA	69, 72, 68, 70	279
		2. PETER THOMSON	AUSTRALIA	73, 67, 70, 70	282
		3. ERIC BROWN	BUCHANAN CASTLE	67, 72, 73, 71	283

19th	1960	1. KEL NAGLE	AUSTRALIA	69, 67, 71, 71	278
		2. ARNOLD PALMER	USA	70, 71, 70, 68	279
		3. ROBERTO DE VICENZO	MEXICO	67, 67, 75, 73	282

20th	1964	1. TONY LEMA	USA	73, 68, 68, 70	279
		2. JACK NICKLAUS	USA	76, 74, 66, 68	284
		3. ROBERTO DE VICENZO	ARGENTINA	76, 72, 70, 67	285

21st	1970	1. JACK NICKLAUS	USA	68, 69, 73, 73	283
		2. DOUG SANDERS	USA	68, 71, 71, 73	283
		Play off	NICKLAUS 72		
			SANDERS 73		
		3. LEE TREVINO	USA	68, 68, 72, 77	285

22nd	1978	1. JACK NICKLAUS	USA	71, 72, 69, 69	281
		2. SIMON OWEN)	NEW ZEALAND	70, 75, 67, 71	283
		RAYMOND FLOYD)	USA	69, 75, 71, 68	
		BEN CRENSHAW)	USA	70, 68, 73, 71	
		TOM KITE)	USA	72, 69, 72, 70	

23rd	1984	1. SEVE BALESTEROS	SPAIN	69, 68, 70, 69	276
		2. BERNHARD LANGER)	GERMANY	71, 68, 68, 71,	278
		TOM WATSON) USA		71, 68, 66, 73	

24th	1990	1. NICK FALDO	ENGLAND	67, 65, 67, 71	270
		2. MARK MCNULTY)	USA	74, 68, 68, 65	275
		PAYNE STEWART)	USA	68, 68, 68, 71	

25th	1995	1. JOHN DALY	USA	67, 71, 73, 71,	282
		CONSTANTINO ROCCA	ITALY	69, 70, 70, 73	282
		Daly wins four-hole play-off			
		3. STEVEN BOTTOMLEY	ENGLAND	70, 72, 72, 69	283

26th	2000	1. TIGER WOODS	USA	67, 66, 67, 69	269
		2. ERNIE ELS)	S. AFRICA	66, 72, 70, 69	277
		THOMAS BJORN)	DENMARK	69, 69, 68, 71	

27th	2005	1. TIGER WOODS	USA	66, 67, 71, 70	274
		2. COLIN MONTGOMERY	SCOTLAND	71, 66, 70, 72	279
		3. FRED COUPLES	USA	68, 71, 73, 68	280

Another day dawns on the Old Course.

James Braid, the double winner at St Andrews in 1905 and '10, finishing a round of 74 aged 78!

In a statement released 6 months after the Open Championship played at St Andrews in 2005, the R & A announced that the economic turnover for the events staged in the "Home of Golf" was £72 million + !

World wide TV coverage by 47 broadcasting companies covering 194 territories had accrued £40 million that year; - local caddie, Tom Kidd, was delighted with his windfall of £11 money prize and the publicity he gained the next week in the local paper, after winning the first Open at St Andrews in 1873!!